THE BUDDHIST SWASTIKA AND HITLER'S CROSS

"The Reverend Dr. T.K. Nakagaki renders a great service by rescuing the swastika, or manji, a benign 1,400-year-old Buddhist symbol in Japan, from its hateful use by Adolf Hitler and his fascist Nazi thugs. It is must reading for all who care about the healing impact of the world's great religions."

Dr. George Packard, Dean Emeritus, Johns Hopkins School of Advanced International Studies

"The Reverend Dr. T.K. Nakagaki has long been a prominent leader in the interfaith movement in New York City, and this book is a further expression of his belief that mutual understanding can lead to enhanced harmony and peace in this world. In a brave gesture of cross-cultural significance, *The Buddhist Swastika and Hitler's Cross* offers us a detailed explanation of the positive history and meaning that this profound symbol has had for millions of people over the millennia."

Rande Brown, LCSW, former Executive Director of the Tricycle Foundation, publisher of *Tricycle: The Buddhist Review*

"Reverend Toshikazu Kenjitsu Nakagaki has shown intellectual courage and integrity in selecting for his book the controversial symbol of the swastika, stigmatized in the West for its association with ideas of racism and hatred and revered in the East for ages as representing a sacred spirituality. He has done a commendable job in presenting his extensive study and research opening the door for the inquisitive to the significance of this many-faceted icon and its implications for peace and reconciliation in today's complex world. The book is undoubtedly impressive and deserves wider global attention and readership."

Ambassador Anwarul K. Chowdhury, Under-Secretary-General of the United Nations (2002–2007)

The Buddhist Swastika and Hitler's Cross

Rescuing a Symbol of Peace from the Forces of Hate

T. K. Nakagaki

Stone Bridge Press • *Berkeley, California*

Published by
Stone Bridge Press
P. O. Box 8208, Berkeley, CA 94707
sbp@stonebridge.com • www.stonebridge.com

This is a redesigned edition of a work privately published in 2017 under the same title.

Front cover design by Linda Ronan incorporating an enhancement of a photograph by Austin Davis Holiday.

First edition 2018. First digital print edition 2023.

Printed in the United States of America.

p-ISBN: 978-1-61172-045-7
e-ISBN: 978-1-61172-933-7

To all those who lost their precious lives by war and violence in the world

Contents

Acknowledgments

The year 2011, when I started my research for this book, was an unforgettable year for me and for many around the globe. The Japanese earthquake and tsunami took away at least 19,000 lives and destroyed the Fukushima Dai-Ichi nuclear complex creating enormous radiation contamination in Japan, causing more suffering. Meanwhile on the other side of the earth, the tenth anniversary of another tragedy, the 9/11 terrorist attack, was commemorated.

The same year also marked the 2,600th anniversary of the Buddha's birthday. It was also the 750th memorial year of the death of Shinran Shonin, the founder of my lineage, Jodoshinshu (True Pure Land) Buddhism, and the 800th memorial year for Honen Shonin, the teacher of Shinran and founder of Jodo (Pure Land) Buddhism.

In 2011, I visited for the first time the Auschwitz and Treblinka death camps in Poland. I felt much sadness during these visits, but I was so grateful to have an opportunity to pay my respects to the victims of the Holocaust, or *Shoah*.

I would like to dedicate this book to mark all of the above happenings of 2011 and all the lives that were lost by these tragic events.

From mid-2016, with the beginning of the Trump presidential campaign, hate crimes have increased and the swastika symbols is being used more and more as a hate symbol and as a symbol by neo-Nazi groups. It is always sad for me to see people using this sacred symbol for hate crimes. This continued to increase in 2017 after Donald Trump became the US president.

This book could not have been completed without the support and encouragement of many individuals. I would like to express my deep appreciation to the following:

First, I would like to thank Mr. Peter Goodman of Stone Bridge Press for his support in the publication of this book. As this work grew out of my doctoral dissertation for New York Theological Seminary, I want to express my gratitude to my NYTS advisors: Dr. Dale Irvin, Dr. Wanda

Lundy, and Dr. Jerry Reisig, and to my site team members: Dr. Karim Abdul-Matin, Rabbi Jo David, Greta Elbogen, Naresh Jain, Dr. M. G. Prasad, and Dr. Matt Weiner. I feel fortunate to have such individuals who gave me detailed advice for my book: Philip Getz, Dr. Leo Lefebure, Dr. Aimee Light, Dr. Jennifer Peace, and Dr. Madhuri M. Yadlapati. I appreciate my wonderful friends and colleague who sent blurbs for this book (listed here in alphabetical order): Rande Brown, Ambassador Anwarul Chowdhury, Dr. Dale Irvin, Dr. Leo Lefebure, Dr. George Packard, Rabbi Michael Schudrich, and Dr. Robert Thurman. My special thanks go to my wife, Heather Harlan Nakagaki, for her constant support and encouragement and for the many hours she patiently spent helping me with revisions.

I would like to share poetry and words that have inspired and guided me throughout my work on this subject. The following is a quote from Holocaust survivor Greta Elbogen's poem, "Remember Me!"

"Not In My Dictionary"[1]

In my dictionary the word
Disgusting
Is replaced with
The unique nature of things.
The word
Hate
Is replaced with
Inquiry into the unfamiliar.
Instead of
Revenge
Is stated
Dialogue with the one who hurt me.
In place of the word
War
Is written,
*Building bridges of understanding
Between myself and the other.*

I was further encouraged by these words from the Hasidic Jewish master, Rebbe Nachman of Breslow (1772–1810):[2]

Know! A person walks in life on a very narrow bridge. The most important thing is not to be afraid.

The highest peace is the peace between opposites. If you remember this the next time you meet someone who makes you uncomfortable, instead of heading for the nearest exit, you'll find ways for the two of you to get along.

To be a person of truth, be swayed neither by approval nor disapproval. Work at not needing approval from anyone and you will be free to be who you really are.

Develop a good eye. Always looking for good will bring you to truth.

Truth is the "light" by which to find your way out of darkness. Turn it on.

If you believe that you can damage, then believe that you can fix. If you believe that you can harm, then believe that you can heal.

Thank you, and may all living beings be happy, well, and peaceful. May we all be free from the attachment of greed, anger, and ignorance. May we all attain enlightenment.

T. K. Nakagaki

Western vs. Eastern Perceptions of the Swastika

More than eleven million men, women, and children were murdered during the Holocaust between 1933 and 1945 by Hitler's Nazi regime. This number includes approximately six million Jews[3]—two thirds of all Jews in Europe at the time. Five million human beings from other groups, including Gypsies, Russian prisoners of war, the handicapped, Hitler's political and religious opponents, Jehovah's Witnesses, blacks, and homosexuals were also killed. This genocide was carried out under the Nazi flag, which featured a symbol that is known in the West as the swastika, forever associating that symbol in Western eyes with evil, death, and destruction.

Even today, 70 years after the end of World War II, the symbol has continued to be used frequently, in Europe, the United States, and other countries to express hatred toward Jews, Muslims, and immigrants. In February of 2015, during one month alone, the following incidents occurred: In France, swastikas were scrawled on overturned and broken tombstones in incidents at three separate Jewish cemeteries. At one of the graveyards, about 300 headstones were damaged, and some were sprayed with swastikas.[4] In a Jewish neighborhood in Montreal, Canada, someone painted red swastikas on several cars at an indoor garage. Envelopes containing a bullet and a note threatening "You're going to get one of these in your head" were left on the windshields of the vehicles.[5] In San Diego, California, swastikas along with profanity and white supremacist graffiti were sprayed on the walls of a high school.[6] In Washington State, a Hindu temple was vandalized with a swastika and a message that said "Get Out," shortly before the temple, which has been there for two decades, was to celebrate a major traditional festival. At a nearby junior high school, a swastika along with the message "Get Out Muslims" was found written on a wall the same day, scrawled by the same perpetrator authorities believe.[7]

In much of Asia, however, particularly in the Buddhist, Hindu, and Jain traditions, the symbol represents something entirely and ironically different. There it is a sacred spiritual symbol of good luck, auspiciousness, and peace and has been for thousands of years. In these traditions, the swastika represents divinity, the cycle of rebirth and liberation from suffering. Asians do not associate it with the Nazis. Many are not even conscious of what the symbol has come to represent in Europe and America as a result of the Nazis' hijacking of it. It is important to understand that Hitler's version of the swastika, as well as the definition of the term "Aryan," was his own systematic construction used for propaganda purposes to further his anti-Semitic political agenda. This construction was not a simple appropriation of a foreign symbol. For Hitler, it was more essentially a variation on the Christian cross symbol, a kind of anti-Semitic cross.

The symbol of the swastika has since the 20th century become so conflated with evil, Hitler, and anti-Semitism that its ancient origins and continued positive benevolent meanings for Buddhists, Hindus, Jains, and others that exist aside from Hitler's distortion and desecration have been lost or banished from contemporary conversation.

While we must be cautious to never forget the history of the swastika's usage by Hitler and others as an instrument of evil, we must also beware of *permanently* reassigning this Western meaning to the symbol in a way that silences Asian tradition. The symbol's historical and ongoing negative usage as a tool to murder, intimidate, and threaten is very real and cannot be erased. Yet this truth ought not to be allowed to eclipse the equally significant truth of how meaningful it is within Asian cultures, where 2.5 billion people—approximately 1/3 of the world's population—practice religions where it is and has been considered sacred for at least 3,000 years. In Buddhist temples throughout Asia, this symbol prominently appears on statues of the Buddha, altar decorations, prayer books, and other items. There is a need for mutual understanding among those who view it as a symbol of hate and those who see it as a symbol of peace and auspiciousness. Such an understanding is possible because the bridge that connects them is that neither of these communities condones the Nazi usage of the symbol. This project is undertaken with the hope and confidence that both communities have a deep desire for peace and repudiation of the Nazi usage of the symbol, as well as a world in which genocide never happens again.

As a Buddhist, I see the swastika as one of the sacred symbols of the 2,000-year-old Buddhist tradition. It appears on the cover of our sacred texts, statues, and on other ritual and decorative objects as an expression of Buddha's mind and all the good virtues of the universe. For me it is tragic to see that the swastika symbol appears to have been permanently desecrated in the West because of its misappropriation in the past by Nazi Germany, and in the present by racist groups and individuals. Buddhists—as well as members of other Eastern religions, including Hindus and Jains—cannot use the swastika freely in the U. S. because of cultural and social perceptions. The swastika, one of the oldest sacred symbols used by human beings, is still commonly and widely used in Japan and many Asian countries without offense or intent to harm others. The swastika has also in the past been used as a motif and symbol with positive associations in other world traditions including Christianity, Judaism, Islam, and Native American Indian cultures. Given the long history and widespread use of this symbol as a marker of peace across time, place, and religious traditions, it is important to take up the conversation of its meaning and reclaim a deeper understanding of this symbol beyond the narrow and hateful distortion of Hitler's misappropriation of it.

Here, Rebbe Breslow's words appeal to me, saying, "The highest peace is the peace between opposites. If you remember this the next time you meet someone who makes you uncomfortable, instead of heading for the nearest exit, you'll find ways for the two of you to get along."[8]

A Few Notes on Terms and Images

There are different words used in the West to refer to the 卍 • 卐 • 卐 symbol. "Hakenkreuz" is a German word meaning literally, "hook-cross." The commonly used English term "swastika" is derived from the Sanskrit word "svastika." Various other words have been used to refer to the symbol in English language including: *fylfot, gammadion* and *Thor's hammer*. In order to avoid confusion, I will use "swastika" as a general term to refer to the symbol in this book. However, the Sanskrit word "svastika" is used occasionally when referring to the traditional Eastern concept of the symbol. When referring to Hitler's symbol, the German term "Haken-kreuz" or its English translation, "Hook-Cross," is used in keeping with how Hitler himself referred to the symbol. Hitler's symbol is usually tilted 45 degrees, with a right-turning orientation.

My First Encounter in the US with the Western Perception of the Swastika

I served as a Buddhist priest in various temples of the Buddhist Churches of America (BCA) for more than 25 years. There are many sects of Bud-dhism in Japan. My sect, Jodoshinshu, was established by Shinran Sho-nin, a Buddhist teacher who lived from 1173 to 1262. My family's temple, Zenshu-ji, near Osaka, was established in 1045 and originally belonged to a different branch of Buddhism. Shinran was part of a reformist movement in Japanese Buddhism at the time and was the first monk to publicly take a wife and have children. Encouraged by his teacher, Honen, who advocated lay Buddhism, Shinran brought Buddhism out of the nobility and monasteries in Japan where it had previously been practiced exclusively and taught among the common people. Follow-ing government-led modernization efforts in the mid-19th century Meiji era, monks in all Buddhist sects were allowed to marry. In other parts of Asia, monastic Buddhism is still practiced widely. I usually use the word "priest" or "minister" in English to describe my position, because "monk" in English suggests someone who is celibate and lives in a mon-astery. In Japan, a Buddhist priest is considered a position of respect and many, but not all, priests come from family lineages dating back generations.

My first encounter with how the West perceives the swastika hap-pened in April 1986, the second year after I came to the United States from Japan to serve at a Buddhist temple in Seattle. I made a flower shrine for the Buddha's Birthday, the "Hanamatsuri" ceremony. The flower shrine is a central feature of the Hanamatsuri. I arranged chrysanthemum blos-soms in the shape of a swastika on the front roof of the shrine,[9] as this was the tradition I had been taught and practiced in Japan. Suddenly, seeing what I was doing, a Japanese-American member of the temple rushed toward me in a panic, exclaiming, "You cannot do that!" I did not understand what he meant. "What is wrong? It looks pretty," I said. He gave me a quick lesson that the swastika here represents Nazi Germany's killing of six million Jews in the Holocaust (*Shoah*) and anti-Semitism. He also explained to me that racial issues are very sensitive in this country, unlike Japan, which has a more homogenous society. As I listened to the temple member, I came to understand the different meaning of the swastika in this country, and how sensitive and serious it is. After this incident, I did not use the swastika symbol for 25 years. I did not want to cause more pain to Jewish people.

People of Asian descent who live in the US and other Western countries often encounter unexpected experiences related to the swastika symbol due to the huge cultural gap in what the symbol means in the West and East. I myself now live in New York City, where every few months, the swastika ends up in news headlines, most frequently after being scrawled on a synagogue or in a Jewish neighborhood as a symbol of hate. Although Hitler only used the swastika for two decades compared to the symbol's far wider and longer use over thousands of years and many continents, it is Hitler's distortion of the symbol that dominates Western understanding. This is understandable in the wake of the trauma of the Holocaust. It is understandable because this symbol continues to be used by some as shorthand for hate. This is also understandable because the symbol itself has become such a taboo in the West there is a lack of conversation and education about its original meanings. My motivation for writing this book comes from my hope that discussion and education about the swastika's broader and contradictory history and usage can help reduce its use as a symbol of hate and increase understanding about the meaning of the original symbol for millions of peace-loving people, both in the past and today.

Asian communities in the United States, meanwhile, continue to expand and grow. As they do, they bring their cultural traditions—including symbols—with them. In the case of the swastika, this causes misunderstanding and culture clash. A Jain man from India I know who now lives in a New Jersey suburb recounted to me his surprise when a local policeman, noticing a swastika symbol he had placed above his doorway for good luck, advised him to take it down so as not to offend any neighbors. He quickly obliged. In 2012, an Asian American–owned jewelry shop located in a predominantly Jewish neighborhood in Brooklyn made headlines when a local resident noticed it was selling swastika-shaped earrings. The store manager explained to reporters that the shape was a Tibetan symbol of good-luck and that she was offended by demands the store remove the earrings. "These people are ignorant," the manager told the *New York Daily News*. "They shouldn't say anything if they don't know anything about symbols." A local politician quickly went on the attack ridiculing her "nauseating" explanation of what the swastika meant in her culture. "The average person, when they see a swastika, they see it as a symbol of hate. End of story."[10]

But that is not the end of the swastika's story. Nor its beginnings.

For those raised in the West who travel to the East, unexpectedly seeing swastikas all over the place can be a confusing and shocking experience. In Japan, many Buddhist temples—as well as tourist maps marking the site of a Buddhist temple—use the symbol frequently, but with no explanation of the symbol's meaning. Japanese do not see the need for an explanation, because for them, just as it is for the politician described above, their concept of the "average person" does not see the swastika as anything other than a representation of Buddhism and general symbol of good luck. They do not even see it as the same symbol as that used by Hitler, and in the Japanese language, an entirely different word for Hitler's symbol is used.

Why Discuss the Swastika Now?

"The swastika is the universal symbol of hate and evil."

When a speaker at an interfaith retreat on hate crimes I attended in 2009 made this statement, it shocked me as well as other Buddhist, Hindu, and Jain participants.

"What do you mean by *'universal'*?" I asked. "The swastika was a sacred symbol of good fortune for more than 2,000 years before Nazism and still is." When the speaker, who is a recognized expert on hate crimes, said that he did not know anything about the swastika in Eastern countries, I felt disappointment and unease. It is very troubling that even an expert on hate crimes did not know the larger history and original auspicious meaning of the swastika. This ignorance should not be perpetuated, I thought. This narrow and limited perspective is unacceptable for those of us who value and have grown up with the swastika in our religions and cultures, where it is considered a sacred symbol with very positive meanings. Even though this issue had quietly bothered me for 25 years, I believed it was now time to speak out about it.

After I began my research, I felt that I needed to visit Holocaust sites in Europe, to see them with my own eyes, and to feel with all my senses, as well as simply to show my respect by offering prayers and placing incense to those who were killed in the concentration camps. So, in spring, 2011, I visited three different concentration camps: Treblinka Concentration Memorial site, where most of the Jews in Warsaw, estimated at between 850,000 and 1 million people, were sent and killed; Auschwitz–Birkenau Concentration Camp Memorial site, the Nazis' largest death camp where more than 1.1 million people were murdered; and Sachsenhausen Concentration Camp Memorial site, one of the earliest camps and mainly used for political prisoners and opponents of the regime, in Oranienburg (north of Berlin), Germany. Each had its own characteristics of horror. I stood on the very ground where millions of people—men, woman, children, adults, and elderly—lost their lives. All three sites made me feel sadness, unease, and a sense of darkness without light, in contrast to the warm spring days outside the gates. The phrase "Never Again" etched in the stone monument in Treblinka, the first concentration camp I visited, was so powerful. This is what the Holocaust represents, a recognition of one of humanity's darkest chapters, one that should never again be repeated.

All three camps offer a tremendous amount of educational materials about the Holocaust, and I visited various museums at the sites, yet I did not find any explanation of the Nazi Hakenkreuz nor the Eastern swastika in any of them. This increased my sense of responsibility to continue my research and write this book to bring more information about the swastika symbol to the public. This book is my contribution toward further discussion, debate, and dialogue about the symbol. Such conversation may help create greater understanding not only just of the swastika, but also of the larger and related issues of hate crimes, religious symbols, freedom of religious expression, the meaning and power of symbols, and genocide while also creating a deeper understanding of how the holocaust occurred.

The Second Hindu-Jewish Leadership Summit was held in Jerusalem on February 17–20, 2008, initiated by the World Council of Religious Leaders, and hosted by the Chief Rabbinate of Israel with the support of the American Jewish Committee. A part of the joint declaration talked about the swastika symbol.

> The svastika is an ancient and greatly auspicious symbol of the Hindu tradition. It is inscribed on Hindu temples, ritual altars, entrances, and even account books. A distorted version of this sacred symbol was misappropriated by the Third Reich in Germany, and abused as an emblem under which heinous crimes were perpetrated against humanity, particularly the Jewish people. The participants recognize that this symbol is, and has been sacred to Hindus for millennia, long before its misappropriation.[11]

As prominent religious leaders have already recognized the swastika symbol, we need to now extend the understanding expressed in this declaration by educating others.

It is time to begin to talk about the swastika symbol, one of the world's major religious symbols in human history. Multifaith dialogue, which I have been a part of for many years, is all about discussion and educating each other about our differences in an effort toward mutual respect and understanding, no matter how touchy the topic. We need to get past our initial sense of panic at touching this "taboo" and be able to have this discussion.

The swastika is a live, active symbol for millions of people. It is not something that is dead and needs to be resuscitated, revived, or rescued. It exists not just in antiquity but also in the present as a sacred, vibrant sign of goodness throughout many Asian communities. Its later usage as a marker of hate also unfortunately continues into the present long after Hitler's death and the end of the Nazi regime. Neither of these realities can be denied. When it appears as graffiti on the walls of a synagogue, it is meant by the person who scrawled it to signify hatred and violence. Therefore, those who see it as a symbol of hate are not wrong in their interpretation, but they are mistaken in defining it as a "universal" symbol of hate and evil. If this meaning were not still intended by those who use it with an anti-Semitic agenda, the situation would be simpler, and we could then easily say the swastika is not really evil.

The Human Capacity for Atrocity

The two world wars that occurred during the first half of the 20th century resulted in some of the greatest atrocities ever to have been committed by humans against each other. These acts spanned across several continents. The human toll of destruction included 15–20 million military and civilian deaths during WWI and 50–85 million during WWII. These numbers are so great they are almost unimaginable.

The government of Imperial Japan was the aggressor in many wars from the end of the 19th century and through WWII. These included the 1st Sino-Japanese War in 1894–1895, the invasion of Taiwan in 1895, the Russo-Japan War of 1904–1905, WWI, the 2nd Sino-Japanese War from 1937 to 1945, and of course WWII from 1939 to 1945. Atrocities committed by the Japanese military at the direction of its leadership during these conflicts, particularly during WWII and its campaigns in China, are well documented by Japanese and other nations' historians. They include the Nanking Massacre, also known as the "Rape of Nanking," in 1937–1938, during which as many as 300,000 Chinese were killed; the forcible recruitment of as many as 350,000 "comfort women" from Korea and other nations; and the 1941 surprise attack on the Pearl Harbor that resulted in 2,403 Americans killed and 1,178 wounded. POWs held by the Japanese were often abused, starved, and forced to do hard labor and were even eaten in cannibalistic practices.[12] Although the exact total numbers of deaths at the hands of the Japanese military spanning these conflicts vary according to researchers, estimates suggest between 3 and 10 million individuals were killed in Asian countries that Japan invaded and colonized.[13] According to the *Encyclopedia of Genocide*, Imperial Japan killed as many as 5,964,000 individuals between 1936 and 1945.[14] The Japanese native animistic religion of Shintoism was co-opted by the militarists to create a state-sponsored cult to further a sense of patriotism and loyalty to the emperor. Most branches of Japanese Buddhism and influential Buddhist leaders, including Zen as well as my own tradition of Jodoshinshu, also expressed support of imperial militarism, twisting and corrupting Buddhist teachings to excuse killing, even though one of the central tenets of Buddhism is the practice of *Ahimsa*, "no harm to others."

We should not forget what happened in these two world wars in order to prevent similar future tragedies that arise from anger and hatred. Future generations need to know and understand the history of past of wars and democide, and to work for a more peaceful world without killing.

While Japan was responsible for much of the death and destruction that occurred during WWII and in other conflicts, it is also the only country to have experienced the devastation of nuclear war following the dropping of atomic bombs on Hiroshima and Nagasaki by the United States. These two events killed as many as 246,000 people, mostly civilians. Many people passed away in the months after the bombing after suffering the painful acute effects of thermal burns and radiation sickness. The year I was assigned to the New York Buddhist Church, 1994, was also the 50th Year Memorial Year of the Hiroshima atomic bombing. A statue of Shinran Shonin that stands in front of the Church survived the bombing and was sent to New York as a symbol of peace in 1955. The presence of this tragic relic at my temple inspired me to create an annual peace ceremony to commemorate the Hiroshima/Nagasaki bombings and send out a message of world peace free from nuclear weapons. I have met many Hiroshima/Nagasaki survivors through the ceremony and other peace events. I am always very impressed by their courage and sense of mission to share their tragic stories in an effort to create a nuclear free and peaceful world. I have learned many things from them. Mr. Koji Kobayashi, a Hiroshima survivor who has participated in our commemoration, once told me: "Although it is a painful experience, if I don't talk about it, people may forget and might use nuclear weapons again. Then others will have to suffer like me in future generations. It could be my grandchildren. Nobody should experience the same suffering as I experienced. As long as I live, I will continue to share my experience."[15]

His view is now common among Hiroshima and Nagasaki survivors, although right after the war it was not. Telling people you were an atomic bomb survivor often meant difficulties in finding a marriage partner due to fear of genetic damage to future generations. In Japanese, the survivors are known as "Hibakusha," which literally means "those who were affected by the atomic bombs." As the years went by, more and more bravely came forward to share their stories. Though they are getting old, their spirit is young and moves many people. As a Japanese from the only country that has experienced the atomic bombings, and as a Japanese Buddhist from a tradition that once supported Japan's militarism, and as a teacher and representative of a religion whose core tenet is non-violence I feel it is my responsibility to further the effort toward a peaceful and nuclear-free world. This is why I organize and participate in peace events.

Encountering Holocaust Survivors

During my time serving as a priest in Japanese-American BCA temples on the West Coast of the United States in the 80s and early 1990s, I did not have many chances to meet and get to know Jewish Americans. The BCA temples on the West Coast are ethnocentric and generally not engaged in interfaith work. Since my relocation to New York City in 1994, I have met many Jews and have had the opportunity to learn about Jewish religious traditions and culture as well as the Holocaust experience. In 2003, I visited the United States Holocaust Memorial Museum in Washington, DC.[16] I spent two full days there viewing and reading the exhibitions, and watching video presentations. I was chilled by the capacity and potential for human beings to kill millions of people. I felt a similar feeling when I visited the Hiroshima Peace Museum for the first time.

When I first told people in 2010 I wanted to write about the swastika, I was met with very negative reactions among non-Asians. Many tried to talk me out of it. One Jewish friend whom I have worked with on many cross-cultural projects threatened to no longer work with me and said she would block any future projects I wanted to do with any of the UN-related NGOs she works with. When I tried to explain why I thought it was important to talk about the swastika as an interfaith and cross-cultural issue, she interrupted me. "No one cares, no one cares," she kept agitatedly repeating as she shook her head back and forth. She wouldn't listen to anything I had to say. I understood her complete and emphatic opposition more clearly after having visited the Holocaust Memorial Museum.

In May 2010, many Hibakusha from Hiroshima and Nagasaki gathered in New York for the occasion of the Nuclear Non-Proliferation Treaty renewal at the United Nations. I organized several Hibakusha talks at schools and churches and at the Jewish Heritage Museum during their visit. I also organized a discussion between Hibakusha survivors and Holocaust survivors at the Church of St. Paul and St. Andrew. None of the Hibakusha spoke English, yet it was an extraordinary meeting that reached beyond words. Just seeing the survivors together was a moving experience. They met each other with spontaneous hugs and greetings such as "you suffered a lot but you survived!" It was a beautiful scene that I did not expect at all.

Sharing stories is a way to heal wounds. It is both hard to speak about the horrors of WWII and also hard to hear what happened. I always had an image of the Holocaust as a real taboo in this country about which no one should ever speak. Hearing the Holocaust survivors' stories changed this perception. They were open and willing to share their experiences. Like the Hibakusha, they explained that the very reason we should talk more about what they endured is so that nobody else will ever need to go through such a painful experience again. Both the atomic bombings and the Holocaust were once taboo and maybe still are to some degree, but it is now understood that it is necessary to talk about them.

One of the speakers from among the Holocaust survivors who gave me a sense of hope was Greta Elbogen, who was born in Vienna, Austria, and survived the Nazi persecution as a young child in Budapest, Hungary. Her father was taken to various forced slave labor camps, and later to the Dachau concentration camp, where he died in 1945. Her mother, one older sister, and two older brothers survived.

"When I tried to share the story with my grandchildren, my son discouraged me and stopped me from doing so," she said. "It is common for the 2nd and 3rd generation of Jews to oppose the opening up of this discussion." I asked her why she wanted to share her story. She replied that it was to convey the message of "never again"—so that the tragedy will never again happen to any other people. Her response was basically the same as that of Mr. Kobayashi, the Hiroshima survivor.

Greta Elbogen is a psychotherapist, and I interviewed her later when I decided to research the swastika symbol. I asked her opinions about my project. Elbogen's attitude was positive, curious, and enthusiastic, which was a great source of comfort and encouragement, and made it possible for me to continue. All survivors of the Holocaust may not think the same way as Elbogen does, but I felt that sharing stories can be healing for many.

"When I was asked to collaborate on a project of researching the meaning and history of the swastika, I saw it as an excellent opportunity to join a well-known Buddhist faith, interfaith, and peace activist, to use this topic for dialogue among Jews, non-Jews, and Holocaust survivors to ease the reactions to swastikas by widening the meaning of it. Bringing information and talking about it could help release the negative reactions," said Elbogen. "I am committed to healing myself and others to create inner and outer peace. The best way to bring about change is when each individual is working on self-development."

Elbogen continued, "Many people make a big deal about the swastika because they don't know what the swastika means. Many Jewish people don't know that the swastika also has been a good luck symbol for other religions. When a swastika is drawn in Brooklyn or California, if they knew that, they would not be so frightened."[17]

Importance of Dialogue

Talking about the swastika can open dialogue. Such a dialogue can embrace the tragedy of the Holocaust—not forgetting its victims but rather remembering them as the way not to repeat it—while also providing paths to tolerance, respect, and deeper mutual understanding of our religions, cultures, and historical experiences. To do so does not in any way dilute the very real and dark history of the swastika's literally twisted desecration by Hitler as a tool toward his goal of genocide in creating his ideal "Aryan" society.

The purpose of interfaith dialogue is always to create mutual respect and understanding. Through such dialogue the swastika can overcome its desecration, and healing can occur in multiple directions. In this sense, the symbol itself is truly like another Buddhist symbol, the lotus flower, which for Buddhists represents enlightenment through transformation. The lotus grows out of mud—which in Buddhism represents defilement, evil, and difficulties—and then blossoms with pure white flowers. Without mud, there can be no flower of enlightenment. Difficulties and suffering are the source of true enlightenment in Buddhism.

Our Own Monsters Within

Human beings are capable of doing many cruel and destructive acts such as the Holocaust. We need to remind ourselves that these events were tragedies not just for Jews but for all of humanity. It is not about who is good and who is evil, but rather, it is a recognition that we all have the potential to do evil as well as good. Mother Teresa, when asked when she had begun her work of relief and care for abandoned children replied, "on the day I discovered I had a Hitler inside me."[18] We all have a responsibility to identify and bring out into the open our own hatred, discrimination, and ability to bring suffering and pain as displayed throughout human history. Through this process we can also discover our own inner wisdom, and then find inner peace among us. Instead of identifying who is evil, it may be more important to realize the monsters within each of us. When we identify someone as evil, it is not humanity's problem but *their* problem. But this is *our* issue as human beings. Genocide is possible anywhere at any time and will continue as long as humans fail to recognize their own monsters within. As a result of WWII, the swastika, once a worldwide symbol of peace and good will, now as a symbol represents both the sages and monsters within us.

ONE

The Swastika Symbol in My Tradition

Sometimes something is so close that we may fail to see it. There is a Japanese saying, "The lighthouse does not shine on its base." The lighthouse shines far into the distance, yet its base is dark. Our eyes can see people all around us, but we fail to see ourselves who are closer than anyone else. For human beings to live, we need to breathe the air, yet most of the time we are not conscious of our own breath. That which is close is often a blind spot. It is there but not there. It is here but not here. However, once being noticed, it may surprise us a great deal. This is the case with the swastika symbol in the East. It is so ubiquitous, it is usually not even noticed.

The Swastika in Japan

In Japan "manji" is the word used to refer to the swastika. It is derived from the Chinese character for the swastika, "wan," which also means "10,000." The number in this case does not necessarily mean the actual number ten thousand, but rather a sense of a huge number too great to imagine or too many to count. Numbers are often used in Buddhism in this way. When one refers to the Buddha's "ten-thousand virtues," the meaning to be conveyed is that which is great and numberless, beyond that of the ordinary. The swastika arrived in Japan more than 1,500 years ago with the introduction of Buddhism. Since then it has come to be seen in Japan primarily as a Buddhist symbol especially because it is used on maps in Japan to represent the location of Buddhist temples. The swastika was standardized as a temple marker on maps during the Meiji era in the 1880s[19] and has been used since then. All cities, towns, train stations,

1. Swastika symbols marking Buddhist temples on maps in Japan.

and tourist attractions in Japan have maps, and one can easily see swastika symbols on them, as there are about 85,000 Buddhist temples in Japan (Fig. 1). In the ancient capitals, Kyoto and Nara, both of which are famous for their many Buddhist temples, visitors inevitably encounter the swastika symbol.

Although there are many Buddhist institutions such as Buddhist universities in Japan, and many scholars of Buddhism in Japan who have researched and written on the history and teachings of Buddhism, it is rare to find a book or journal article specifically about the swastika symbol. The study of the swastika is a blind spot in Japanese Buddhist studies with few resources available, in spite of its ancient and broad usage in Japan. A two-volume set of books titled *Manji no Hakubutsushi* (Record of the Swastika) written by Manji Uemura, a professor of philosophy and Judaic studies at Kobe Gakuin University, may be the only work in Japanese scholarship which encompasses various aspects of the swastika symbol. The first volume discusses the symbol's history and usage in Japan, and the second volume explains the swastika's use in other countries. The second volume relies heavily on *Swastika: The Earliest Known Symbol and Its Migrations*, written by Thomas Wilson in 1894. For Professor Manji Uemura, his research has been a personal journey as well. His first name, "Manji"—as you may have already suspected—is actually the swastika symbol. Professor Uemura wanted to find the roots of the name his parents gave him when he was born in 1942,[20] he explained to me during a meeting we had in 2010 at his university. In Japan, although the phonetic name "Manji" is a common male name, it is uncommon to write it with the swastika character. The Japanese language has many homonyms and in choosing names there are often many Chinese characters with the same pronunciation from which to choose. The character is what imparts meaning to the name. Professor Uemura said that his parents' choice derives from a classical Japanese poetic expression used to describe a heavy snowfall: "manji tomoe to yuki ga furu." In English: "The snow falls in a whirling swirl." The "manji" here as well as the word "tomoe" (which is a similar shape to the swastika, but with curved arms of three or more) describes the movement of the snow, the sense of "swirling" or "whirling" snowfall changing direction and shape. His sisters' names, Tomoe and Yuki, both typical girls names, are also taken from this phrase. Although Uemura was born in the middle of WWII, his parents apparently did not associate the swastika with Hitler's symbol. This is another example of how Japanese even during WWII differentiated the swastika from Hitler's symbol.

[1] Buddhist Temples with Swastikas

Zenko-ji temple in Nagano, founded in A.D. 642, is Japan's first Buddhist temple. Historically it is also the most important and influential temple in Japan. Its statue of Amida Buddha, which was brought from Korea in 552, is said to be the oldest Buddha statue in Japan. The swastika is extensively used throughout the temple, often alongside the temple's crest design of the hollyhock flower. It is said that Zenko-ji's use of the symbol is more frequent than at any other Buddhist temple in Japan. It can be seen on banners, paper lanterns, iron lanterns, pillars roof tiles, and throughout the main shrine room. This prolific use at Japan's oldest temple shows the sacred value of the swastika from the dawn of Buddhism in the country (Figs. 2–5).

Senso-ji Buddhist temple, also known as the Asakusa Kannon Temple, is another temple in Japan which abundantly uses the swastika. Senso-ji is the most popular and oldest Buddhist temple in Tokyo. Dedicated to Kannon Bodhisattva, the temple dates back to A.D. 645 For 1,300 years, it has been a center of the local community. It is one of Tokyo's major tourist attractions. Swastikas appear on Senso-ji's altar, center roof, roof tiles, containers, incense burners, and candle altar (Figs. 6–8). The symbol can also be found on amulets sold at the temple and on souvenirs such as paper lanterns and change purses sold on Nakamise, the popular shopping corridor in front of the temple.

Kyoto, one of Japan's ancient capitals, holds thousands of Buddhist

2. Zenko-ji Buddhist temple in Nagano. The banner has swastika symbols and standing hollyhock symbols.

3. Swastika and dharma-wheel symbols on the rooftop at Saiho-ji Buddhist temple, built in 1199. It was used as a temporary worship hall for Zenko-ji from 1700 to 1709.

4. Garden lantern at Zenko-ji.

5. Left- and right-turning swastika symbols on pillars at Zenko-ji temple.

6. Roof with swastikas at Senso-ji Buddhist temple in Asakusa, Tokyo.

7. A container with swastika symbol and decorative border at Senso-ji.

8. A huge incense burner with swastika symbol at Senso-ji.

temples representing Japan's dozens of varied lineages. Down almost every street you turn in this city you can find a temple. They come in all sizes and types, each rich with history. Some occupy wide spaces many blocks square with numerous separate buildings or even a whole university within such as the Nishi Hongwan-ji, the head temple for my sect, located along one of Kyoto's major downtown avenues. Although my sect does not use the symbol much in Japan, others do. One of these is Manpuku-ji Zen temple (Fig. 9) located in Uji, Kyoto, founded by a Chinese monk, Ingen, who came to Japan in 1661. Here swastikas can be seen in the lattice woodwork of railings, on a large enamel incense burner, and on other temple decorations.

Many Buddhist temples in Kyoto, including Chugen-ji, Ansho-in, Yata-dera, and Shakuzo-ji, house shrines dedicated to Jizo (*Ksitigarbha*) Bodhisattva (Fig. 10). The swastika symbol usually accompanies Japanese depictions of Jizo and can be seen at these shrines.

Nestled down the winding back streets of downtown Kyoto, one can easily find small roadside shrines to Jizo Bodhisattva in front of homes and businesses (Fig. 11). Known as the protector of travelers, women, children, and unborn babies, Jizo is the most beloved, friendly, and respected Bodhisattva for Japanese Buddhists. There are many folk stories about Jizo helping villagers and children. Statues of Jizo are frequently found at the intersections of country roads and paths throughout Japan. Jizo often is depicted accompanied by a swastika because as an image, it too is seen as warm, kind, and revered in Japan.

I myself never much noticed these and other swastikas that are around me all the time in Japan until I started actively looking for them while doing my research. One day while staying in Kyoto, I asked my American-born wife to please let me know if she saw any swastikas. She laughed and pointed out that we were passing about a dozen of them on Jizo shrines during our daily walk down the backstreets between Kyoto Station and Nishi Hongwan-ji temple. To her as an American they stood out, but I had not noticed them at all—even while doing research on the swastika—on streets that I have walked often since my days as a university student. I decided to see if others had the same reaction. I asked native Kyotoites as well as Buddhism professors from my alma mater, Ryukoku University, if they knew of specific places where I could find swastikas around Kyoto. Most answered with blank stares and replied that it was not something they ever paid much attention to. Yet, they probably pass a Jizo shrine every day. It is something that is always there but is so integrated into the common sights of everyday life in Japan that until someone points it out, is not even noticed.

Although the swastika is more strongly associated in Japan with Buddhism than Shintoism, the symbol can also be found at some Shinto shrines on decorative items such as roof tiles, lanterns, and banners. Examples can be seen at the Nezu shrine and Shoin shrine in Tokyo, and the Togaku shrine in Nagano. Shintosim is a native form of animistic worship that predates the history of Buddhism in Japan. Although the two religions are distinct, over time the Japanese came to see them as syncretic, and most Japanese practice both. Most Japanese have Shinto

9. Swastika railing at Manpuku-ji Zen temple, Kyoto (built in 1661).

10. Swastika Lanterns for "Higiri" Jizo at Ansho-ji Buddhist temple, Kyoto (built in 942).

11. Various Jizo shrines near Kyoto Station.

12. Kimono with swastika pattern.

13. Amulet with swastika emblem.

weddings and Buddhist funerals. Rituals and holidays associated with both religions are commonly observed. Shinto shrines are often found on the grounds of Buddhist temples. It is possible that the appearance of swastikas in Shintoism is due to this historical mixing of the two traditions. In many branches of Japanese Buddhism, Shinto gods are interpreted as incarnations of Buddhas and Bodhisattvas. Another possibility is that the swastikas in these cases derive from the family crests of the priests of those temples. In both Shintoism and Buddhism, temples are passed down through many generations in priestly and aristocratic families. Swastikas are sometimes used in Japanese family crests. Shinto shrines, along with Buddhist temples, often integrate the family crests of the priestly families who own and run them into their decorative designs such as roof tiles.

[2] Various Swastika patterns in Japan

Swastika decorative designs and patterns are also used for many everyday non-religious items in Japan including paper lanterns, socks, wallets, *happi* festival coats, kimonos, and ceramics. This frequent and varied use shows how integrated the symbol is into not just religion but also culture and everyday life in Japan. The swastika is a vital part of Japanese life today not just as a religious symbol but also as a more general symbol of beauty, peace, luck ,and happiness. Figs. 12–17 show this variety of usage.

In Japanese arts and culture, geometric patterns incorporating the swastika are called *Sayagata, Manji Kuzushi,* or *Manji Tsunagi.* These patterns are used for, among other items, kimono fabric, ceramics and

14. Happi festival coat with swastika border.

15. Change purse with swastika.

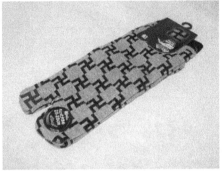

16. Ceramic dishes with swastikas.

17. Tabi socks with swastika design.

architectural motifs. Some of these patterns use the shape in a subtle way, such as *Igeta Manji, Fundo Tsunagi,* and *Mutsute Manji* (Fig. 18). These many types of swastika patterns also came to Japan from China, where they can be seen in many examples of artistic design. These are some swastika patterns frequently found on wood latticework and fabric (Fig. 19).

The swastika is one of many types of graphic designs used for Japanese family crests, known as "Kamon" in Japanese. "Ka" literally means house, family, or lineage (Fig. 20). "Mon" means crest or emblem, and expresses the genealogical connection to a family. *Kamon* designs are classified into several categories including flowers, trees, animals, insects, tools, characters, building shapes, and geometric patterns. Many have been passed down in families for centuries. *Kamon* are also sometimes used as emblems for organizations, as well as towns and cities in Japan.

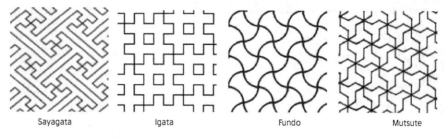

| Sayagata | Igata | Fundo | Mutsute |

18. Various geometric patterns.

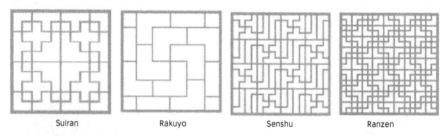

| Suiran | Rakuyo | Senshu | Ranzen |

19. Swastika patterns of wood latticework.

20. Various *kamon* family crest designs.

The swastika has been used as a *kamon* for centuries to express good luck, prosperity, and a connection to Buddhism. It was also sometimes used as a *kamon* by families who secretly practiced Christianity during the 17th-century Edo period, when Christianity was banned in Japan. Because the swastika has a cross in the middle, or is "a single cross with four ends at right and left angles" it was therefore seen as a type of cross.[21]

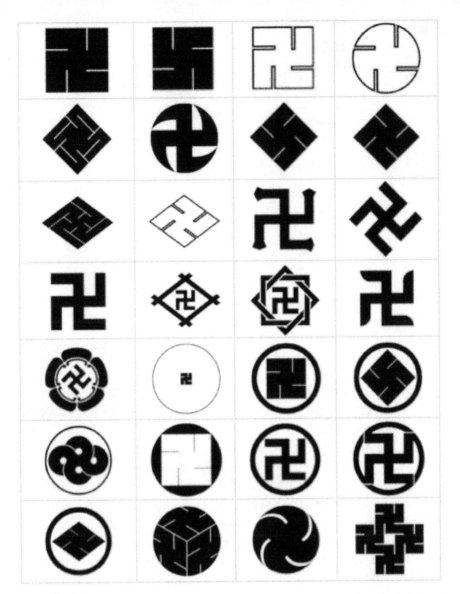

Fig.21. Examples of various swastika family crests found in Japan.

The swastika has therefore been used as both a symbol of Buddhism and Christianity in Japan. There are a number of well-known swastika-design family crests including that of the Hachisuka, Itami, Odagiri, Tada, Tsugaru, Torii, Ono, Okabe, and Hattori families, to name just a few (Fig. 21).

Hirosaki city in Aomori Prefecture, in the northern part of Japan,

22. Pokémon card with red swastika.

uses the Tsugaru family crest as their city emblem. The Japanese artist Yoshitomo Nara, a Hirosaki native, often uses the swastika in his sculptures. Some examples were on view in 2010 at his exhibition "Nobody's Fool" at the Asia Society in New York.[22]

The popular Shorinji Kempo martial arts school originally used a left-oriented swastika as its logo. The founder, So Doshin, created the school as a fusion of Buddhism and Chinese Shaolin self-defense in 1947 with the intent of creating a more peaceful society in the aftermath of the violence of WWII. The logo was changed to a double circle design in 2005 after the school received complaints and criticism when students went abroad for tournaments in Western countries.[23]

Japan is a leader in the field of animated comic books and films or "anime" as they are popularly known. Anime conventions are very popular these days both inside and outside Japan. Swastikas appear in some anime, but when they do they are often erased when shown or exported outside of Japan. Pokémon is a well-known anime figure in Japan and around the world. In December 1999, a controversy ensued after young children in New Jersey discovered swastikas on Pokémon cards they purchased at a local collectables store (Fig. 22). The children were Jewish, and the symbol upset them and their parents. "The whole premise of the game is kids having fun," Steve Weisman, father of a 10-year old who bought the card, told the Associated Press. "This reminded people of 6 million deaths." Nintendo, the manufacturer, said the card was meant for sale only in Japan and not in the US, and was imported without company approval. Nintendo quickly agreed to discontinue the card. The company issued a statement explaining that in Japan the "manji" carries a positive message, although the creators "also understand that there is potential for others to misunderstand the symbol." The statement added, "What is appropriate for one culture may not be for another."[24]

The Anti-Defamation league praised Nintendo's quick decision to pull the card. "We recognize that there was no intention to be offensive, but goods flow too easily from one place to another in the world," said Kenneth Jacobson, a spokesperson for the group. "The notion of isolating it in Asia would just create more problems."[25] From this statement one would think this appearance of the swastika in Japan was an isolated instance, when in fact it is commonplace. Such a statement reveals a Western-centric attitude and complete ignorance of the importance and prevalence of the symbol, as well as a need to educate Western countries about the symbol.

In the popular Japanese anime series *Bleach*, the characters' special transformation into superheroes is called "Ban-Kai" which is written in Japanese as 卍解. *Ban* is an alternate reading of the manji character, meaning fulfillment, and *Kai* means to release. Episodes of *Bleach* often contain scenes where the swastika figures prominently, such as one where the main hero, Ichigo Kurosaki, holds a swastika to recover his hero powers.[26]

Blade of the Immortal (1994), an award-winning anime, has a samurai warrior main character named "Manji" who wears a black and white kimono with a large swastika. The English-language version, published by Dark Horse Comics, includes a section called "About the Translation" with an explanation of the swastika. It says:

> It is important that readers understand that the swastika has ancient and honorable origins and it is those origins that apply to this story which takes place in the 18th century (ca. 1782–3). There is no anti-Semitic or pro-Nazi meaning behind the use of the symbol in this story. Those meanings did not exist until after 1910.[27]

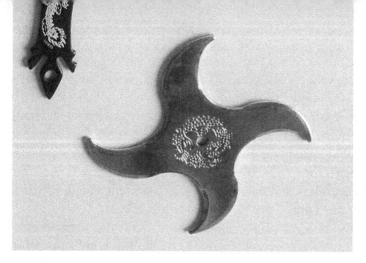

23. Manji (swastika-shaped) Shuriken used by ninja.

Katsushika Hokusai (1760–1849) was a Japanese Ukiyo-e painter and printmaker of the Edo period. In 1834, after turning 75 years old, he adopted the pen name, "Gakyo Rojin Manji" (画狂老人卍), meaning "old man Manji-mad with painting."[28] On his gravestone in Asakusa, Tokyo, this epithet is carved into the stone. Hokusai was also a fine pattern designer. Many swastika patterns can be found in his book "Notes of New Shapes and Small Patterns (Shingata Komoncho)."[29] Manjiro Hokuga 卍楼北鵞, a disciple of Hokusai, used the swastika as a part of his pen name.

There are many other Japanese historical figures whose names contained the manji-swastika. They include Buddhist monks: Mangai 卍凱, Manzan Dohaku 卍山道白, Mangen Shihan 卍元師蛮, Mankai Sosan 卍海宗珊, Manan Shigan 卍庵士顔, and Jido Kakuman 字堂覚卍; a poet: Nishigaki Manzenshi 西垣卍禅; and even a few legendary ninja: Manji-Gama no Kurodo 卍鎌の蔵人, Manji Kamaitachi 卍かまいたち, Manji Maru 卍丸.

Junichiro Tanizaki (1886–1985) is one of the major writers of modern Japanese literature and a well-known novelist. One of his novels, "卍" (Manji), published in 1928, explored lesbianism. Several films using the title "卍" that were based upon the novel were made in 1964, 1983, 1998 ,and 2006 in Japan. However, when the book was translated into English in 1994 the title was changed to "Quicksand."[30]

The swastika as a name or descriptive term is quite common in Japan. It can be found in the name of a restaurant such as the Chuka Ramen

Manji 中華ラーメン卍 noodle shop in the city of Sendai. It is part of the name of a wrestling technique (Manji Gatame 卍固め) and samurai techniques to kill (Yagyu-ryu Manji-Sappo 柳生流卍殺法, Nemuri Kyoshioro Manji-Giri 眠狂四郎卍斬り). Japanese little boys pretending to be ninjas toss "Manji Shuriken," throwing stars in the shape of a swastika (Fig. 23). When playing with more modern toys, they can find manji in computer games such as Tengai Makyo II, sold only in Japan, whose main character is named Manjimaru 卍丸.

From the distant past of Japanese history going back hundreds of years of classical arts and religious tradition to the modern activities of videogames and anime, manji have traveled a long and winding path throughout Japanese culture.

Meaning of the Swastika in the Japanese Language

In Japanese culture, the swastika as symbol has a positive meaning deeply connected to Buddhism. This is very clear in how it is used in the culture, and also in how it is defined in Japanese dictionaries as a word-symbol. Here are some examples:

Kojien Japanese Dictionary says:[31]

> Manji【卍・卐】(Meaning of 万字) 1. (Sanskrit word *svastika*, hair on the chest of Vishnu) meaning fulfillment of virtues. It is drawn on the chest of the Buddha as a feature of auspiciousness and all virtues. There are both right-turning and left-turning manji. Buddhism in our country uses mainly left-turning, and it is also used as an icon of Buddhist temples. 2. Shape like 卍. 3. Name of family crests. Things formed of 卍. Left Manji・Right Manji・Sharp Corner Manji・Circular Manji etc.[32]

Nippon Kokugo Daijiten (Dictionary of Japanese Language) explains:

> MANJI【卍、卍字、万字】[n.] 1. Sign of auspiciousness from hair on the chest of Vishnu-god in India originally. It is a feature of auspiciousness and all virtues that appears on the Buddha and Bodhisattva's chest, hands, and legs. In Japan, it is used for Buddhist temple's sign and mark. 2. Shape like 卍. 3. One of family crests. Things formed of 卍. Various kinds of left 卍, right 卐, and circular 卍.[33]

Daikanwa-jiten (Great Chinese-Japanese Dictionary) by Tetsuji Morohashi says:

> 【卍】 read as 'ban' 'man' :
>
> (In Buddhism) Feature of auspiciousness in India. Manji. In Sanskrit, it is called 'Srivatsa' or 'Svastika,' meaning auspicious ocean-cloud, existing joy, happiness. It is an auspicious sign on the Buddha's chest. Chinese sutra-translators used [man] based upon a meaning of gathering all the good virtues and fortunes.
>
> (In Japan) Situation that things are chaotically coming in.
>
> (Reference) Many manji are right turning 卐, but now we follow the Kosho's dictionary. Right turning 卐 is called [migi manji]; when showing the respect to the Buddha, people go around three times with right turns.
>
> Buddha's "Byakugo" (white hair on the central forehead) is circling right. Therefore it is 卐, and 卍 hidari manji (left turn) is wrong in ancient times.[34]

Daijiten (Dictionary of Characters) says:

> 【卍】 Manji: Buddhism uses this sign from ancient times. It is called Svastika, which means the place where all good auspicious virtues gather. It is taught as a seal of the Buddha's Heart. Because this character has the meaning of "all virtues," it became the character "wan" in China.[35]

Bonwa Daijiten (Sanskrit-Japanese Dictionary) defines the *svastika* as:

> Svastika a poet who sings (rare); seal of good fortune; Manji symbol (卍); crossing arms before one's chest; a kind of cross-shaped sweet snacks; sitting with crossed legs.[36]

The world-renowned Buddhist scholar Hajime Nakamura explains in his Buddhist Dictionary, *Bukkyogo Daijiten*:

> 【卍字】 Manji   It originally symbolizes a rare wondrous sign of circulating hair on the chest of the ancient Indian god

known as Vishnu (Krishna). Later in Buddhism (and Jainism), it indicated good luck and auspiciousness, appearing on the chest, hands, feet, and head-hair of the Buddha (or Jain). It also symbolizes the mind of the Buddha. In Japan, it has been used as a sign, emblem, symbol of Buddhism and Buddhist temples.[37]

These definitions and explanations of the manji-swastika are all positive meanings inextricably connected to Buddhism, which has been a major religion in Japan since the end of the 7th century.[38] According to the above definitions, the symbol comes from the Sanskrit term "svastika" which expresses good fortune and auspiciousness. It arrived in Japan along with other sacred symbols of Buddhism, and eventually spread into Japanese culture and daily life. Japanese dictionaries do not include Hitler's swastika in their definitions. Japanese dictionaries have a different word, "haaken kuroitsu,"[39] written in katakana, Japanese phonetic symbols used for foreign loanwords, or "kagi juji" (hook cross),[40] written with the three Chinese characters which together mean "hook" and "cross" for the *Hakenkreuz* (Hook-Cross) swastika of Nazi Germany. The Japanese *manji* is almost always a left-turning swastika, and the Hook-Cross is always a right-turning swastika. The Buddhist swastika in general, not only in Japanese Buddhism but also in Buddhism in other countries such as China, Korea, and Tibet, is standardized as a left-turning swastika.

Meaning of the Swastika in the Buddha's Discourse

What did the Buddha himself say about the swastika? Sutras are the most important scriptures in Buddhism.[41] They are considered the recorded words of the Shakyamuni Buddha, the historical Buddha. There are seven different usages or meanings that the Buddha refers to in various sutras when discussing the swastika symbol.

The symbol is primarily described as one of the thirty-two special features of a Buddha, physical characteristics that mark an enlightened being as different from ordinary beings. In Buddhism, Shakyamuni is not the only "Buddha." Anyone who is enlightened or fully awakened is considered a Buddha.

There are many examples from the Buddhist sutras describing these thirty-two features and the swastika in particular. One example, the

24. Chinese scroll used for a Blessing Ceremony by the American Buddhist Confederation in November 2015.

25. Right-turning swastika on Amida Buddha's chest at Anrakuju-in Buddhist temple in Kyoto.

Agama Sutra, says: "The chest (of the Buddha) has the swastika symbol."[42] Among the mentions of the swastika in the various sutras, the description of the swastika on the Buddha's chest appears the most frequently. Statues in China, Korea, Tibet, Vietnam, and Japan usually depict the Buddha with a swastika on the chest (Figs. 24, 25).

In Japan it appears less often in depictions of the Buddha made after the 15th century. Some of Japan's most famous and oldest works of Buddhist art do feature the swastika on the Buddha's chest. In Nara, Japan's ancient capital, it can be seen on the chest of the 7th-century Medicine Buddha statue at Yakushi-ji temple, a UNESCO World Heritage Site, and on the 8th-century Vairocana Buddha etchings on the bronze lotus base of the Great Buddha statue at Todai-ji temple. In Kyoto the Amida Buddha statue at Anrakuju-in temple, and the nine Amida Buddha statues of Joruri-ji temple, all dating from the 12th century, also have swastikas on the chest. The former is designated in Japan as an Important Cultural Property, while the latter nine statues are listed as National Treasures.

The swastika is also described as one of eighty additional markers of a Buddha in other sutras. For example, *The Sutra of the Collection of the Original Acts of the Buddha* says: "The (Buddha) child's hair is circular, right turning like the swastika."[43] The sutra also says: "Swastika characters appear on the tips of the ten fingers (of the Buddha)."[44] *The Sutra of Great Adornments* states: "His hair has five swastika characters."[45] *The*

26. Buddha with swastika hair.

27. Footprint of the Buddha Sikri, Pakistan (2nd–3rd century A.D.).

28. Buddha's Footprint at Daigyo-ji temple, Kyoto.

Sutra of the Collection of the Original Acts of the Buddha also says: "Bodhi-sattva (Buddha) lifted up his hand with the swastika fortunate sign of a hundred thousand virtues, and conveyed fearlessness."[46] *The Sutra of the Causes from the Past and Present* and *Great Prajna Paramita Sutra* refer to seven parts of the Buddha's body which "on the soles of both feet, on both hands, on both shoulders and on the back of the head clearly feature the swastika."[47]

In these sutras, as well as in artistic depictions of the Buddha, the swastika appears not only on the Buddha's chest, but also on his head, hands, and feet (Figs. 26–28). When found on the hands and feet, the swastika often can be seen together with the Dharma-wheel and the lotus flower. Among Buddhist symbols, the lotus, Dharma-wheel, and swastika are the three most frequent and important symbols.

The *Sutra of the Practice and Original Raising* is one of many that describe the swastika as a visual manifestation of the Buddha's virtue and therefore a lucky and auspicious symbol. It says, "The swastika shows the Buddha's virtues in the world."[48]

Other sutras echo this description:

> "The swastika on the Buddha's chest shows the figure of benefit and virtues."[49]

> "Both the front and back of the swastika have auspicious and lucky figures."[50]

> "Within the swastika sign, revealing the practices with the Buddha's 84,000 virtues..."[51]

> "The swastika is named as the sign of the fulfillment status ... Once one gains this sign, he or she is not afraid of birth and death, and is free from five kinds of greed."[52]

> "The swastika[53] means the entire goodness of the Dharma and the essence of the teachings. In secular society, the evil committed people are 'half' people, and people of good conduct are 'full' people."[54]

According to these sutras, the swastika symbol contains all the virtue, goodness, good luck, and auspiciousness of the Buddha, because the swastika belongs to sacred or holy ones who realize the truth and share it with supreme wisdom and compassion. Such beings are considered noble, a concept expressed in the Buddhist term "Aryan," which like the swastika symbol has also been widely misunderstood in the West because of Hitler's misuse of it.

The swastika is described in sutras as the symbol of a great person, one who overcomes suffering and the sorrow of birth-and-death and reaches the stage of enlightenment through noble actions. A "great person" is one who lives such a noble life. "Great person" is one of several set descriptive phrases including "enlightened one" and Tathagata (one who comes from the truth) and "world honored one" commonly found in the sutras. "The swastika on a Buddha's chest is the mark of a great person,"[55] says the *Sutra of the Precious Woman's Questions*, while the *Sutra of the Dharma-Gate of Pure Practice* says, "The Tathagata Buddha gains the feature of a great person whose chest has the swastika."[56]

The character "dai" in "dai nin" (great person) literally means "big," "broad," "great," and "many," which is the opposite of "small," "narrow," "low," and "few." A person who experiences the world of enlightenment beyond human calculation gains a broader view with great wisdom and compassion and possesses many virtues. These are the qualities of the Buddha that the swastika is meant to represent. Most human beings are caught up in the narrow mind of greed, anger, and our self-centered view, which is small and limited. Things created based upon greed, anger, and delusion have small virtues or may instead bring harm and damage without true wisdom and compassion.

Several sutras associate the swastika with light, which itself is a symbol of Buddhist wisdom:

> "From the swastika diamond-like adornment in his heart, spreads a great bright light."[57]

> "At that time, the Tathagata (Buddha) exposed the treasure-like light from the swastika on his chest. That light has a hundred thousand colors, and illuminated all the Buddha's worlds spreading like particles throughout ten quarters."[58]

> "Those who see the light swastika of Buddha's chest will remove their one hundred twenty trillion sins of birth-and-death."[59]

The exact origin of the swastika is uncertain, as it is such an ancient symbol. However, many scholars believe that the swastika's original meaning was somehow related to the sun and that it was perhaps used by early sun worshipers. It has been found in some ancient cultures alongside other sun symbols.[60] Sun is related to light. When the swastika is understood as a symbol of light, we see the connection between the original meaning of the sun and the swastika light of the Buddha. In Buddhism, light is often a metaphor for wisdom, as the light of wisdom breaks the darkness of ignorance. Therefore, the words of the Buddha or the teachings of the Buddha are symbolized by light.

The swastika also appears in the sutras as a symbol of the Buddha's Heart-Mind, the mind of great compassion, which embraces all beings without discrimination beyond likes and dislikes. According to the *Ocean-Like Sutra on Samadhi through Meditation on the Buddha*:

> "The World Honored One (Buddha)'s rare and great chest symbol (swastika) expresses immeasurable meanings. So as the Buddha's mind possesses the various virtues."[61]

> "One enters the heart of the Bodhisattva through the swastika."[62]

The swastika is described in some sutras as appearing on emblems that adorn the Bodhi tree of the Amitabha Buddha. The Bodhi tree is an important symbol in Buddhism, as the historical Buddha is believed to have achieved enlightenment by sitting underneath one.

> "That Bodhi-tree is ... adorned with the emblems of the dolphin, the swastika, the Nandyavarta and the moon, adorned with nets of jewels and of bells ..."[63]

> "... For in case that the Buddhas of ten quarters immediately come to give to his/her hand, placing beads on a hand; for in case achievement of all the great voice and sound, placing the treasure-bell on a hand; for in case verbal expressions are skillful and clear, placing the treasure-seal (swastika) on a hand; for in case, good gods and dragon king always come and protect, placing treasurer-weapon on a hand ..."[64]

Many different types of symbols are used in Buddhism, particularly in esoteric Buddhism. The above passages are related to various symbols that some Pure Land Buddhist sutras refer to, and to symbolic items held by the Bodhisattva Avalokitesvara with eleven faces and a thousand arms, seen in the photo below (Fig. 29). The Bodhisattva carries a square-shaped swastika seal. True enlightenment is beyond form, and therefore, one symbol is not enough to grasp the world of enlightenment. Many symbols are used to reach enlightenment. Through these symbols we go beyond words, forms, and dualistic thoughts.

Treatises and commentaries of the sutras tend to be longer than the sutras themselves and often have more detailed explanations about the swastika. The following are some examples:

> "In Sanskrit, it (卍) is read 'Srivatsa'; In Chinese, it is a feature

29. Bodhisattva Avalokiteshvara carries the right-turning swastika seal at Koryu-ji Buddhist temple in Kyoto.

of auspiciousness ... it appears several places on the Buddha's (Tathagata's) body, it means good fortune and is the feature of great happiness and virtues."[65]

"The *swastika* means virtuous nature without blind passion. It is the existence of happiness and joy. Therefore, it is the feature of excellent virtue of auspicious happiness. Those who have this feature always receive peace and joy, and live a life twice as long as others. Who controls this symbol creates peace in the center of the heaven, just like the shape of the character."[66]

Most of these explanations are similar to dictionary entries that are meant to define the term, while also adding more interpretations. All similarly define the swastika as a noble symbol in Buddhism, giving longevity, peace, and joy to people and the world. Even in the shorter definitions, the association of enlightenment with the symbol is clearly conveyed:

"Showing the swastika means thousands of virtues and good fortune on the surface, and diamond-like wisdom and determination within."[67]

"The character 卍 should be interpreted as the auspicious ocean-cloud."[68]

"(Buddha's) chest has a swastika which is named as the sign of true form, and spreads Great Light."[69]

The following sutra commentaries dramatically go beyond simple definitions as they portray the symbol itself almost coming to life with its own supernatural ability.

"From the swastika character on the chest, countless hundred thousand million fighting kings appear, and with inconceivable miraculous power, shake a hundred thousand worlds. The brave and strong swastika is pure and cool (like water). In the midst of fighting beings, it bravely makes efforts to shake and destroy the evil army of blind passions (greed, anger and self-centered ignorance)."[70]

"The Bodhisattva spread out a great light from the diamond-like swastika chest adorned with great virtue, that is called the destroyer of demon-hatred. There are billions of lights for family and relatives, already spreading and shining upon the immeasurable world of the entire universe. Showing the infinite divine power, again they enter the Diamond-like swastika chest adorned with great virtue."[71]

In Buddhist texts, 卍 is always defined as the Sanskrit term "svastika." The symbol always means "positive" and is always related to the Buddha's enlightenment. It therefore, expresses happiness, joy, good fortune, and auspiciousness. Because the Buddha has attained true diamond-like wisdom, free from the blind passions of greed, anger, and ignorance, the sign of true happiness of all virtues appears on his/her chest. The swastika is the symbol of this enlightenment. It expresses the Buddha's ability to illuminate all beings with compassion, true happiness and peace.

The Standard Buddhist Swastika Is Left-Turning

The swastika in Buddhism is usually defined as a left-turning, or counter-clockwise swastika, though the sutras always refer to it as right-turning, or clockwise. The ancient Chinese character for the swastika was left-turning. According to the Japanese Buddhist encyclopedia *Bukkyo Daijiten*, the left-turning swastika was formalized in China as the correct way to depict the symbol in 639 at the time of the Tang

Dynasty emperor Wu Zetian. It is not clear why the character became standardized with that orientation. In ancient times, China was the most influential Buddhist region, from where Buddhism eventually spread to Korea, Japan, Vietnam, and Tibet. The left-turning swastika traveled with Buddhism to these countries and generally became standardized in that direction. This is the opposite orientation of the right-turning Nazi Hook-Cross.

The Encyclopedia of Tibetan Symbols and Motifs by Robert Beer describes the direction of the Tibetan Buddhist swastika in relation to the Bon religious tradition. It says:

> In the Tibetan Bon tradition the swastika (Tib. *g.yung drung*) means eternal and unchanging, essentially corresponding to the Buddhist term vajra (diamond-like), and likewise gives its name to the Bonpo tradition. The Bon swastika rotates in an anti-clockwise direction, unlike the Hindu, Jain, and early Buddhist swastika, whose sacred motion is clockwise. For this reason practitioners of the Bonpo tradition circumambulate sacred buildings or pilgrimage sites in an anti-clockwise direction.[72]

Correspondingly, according to Buddhist sutras and in some Buddhist practices such as the Theravada tradition, one shows respect by uncovering the right arm and holding that arm toward the sacred building or statue when walking around it. Bon practitioners believe that according to this practice, the swastika should be clockwise as was originally described in Buddhist sutras.

Though the Buddhist swastika was standardized in China as having a counter-clockwise orientation, clockwise-turning swastikas can still be found in many branches of Buddhism around the world. Although most swastikas found in Japan are left-turning, many of the swastika symbols on the chest of Buddha statues and paintings in Japan, including swastikas appearing in the depictions of the Bodhisattva Avalokitesvara and the ancient artworks of Nara and Kyoto mentioned earlier are, in fact, right-turning. Sometimes both versions of the swastika appear together, such as in depictions of the symbol on the underside of the toes of the Buddha (Figs. 27, 28). Lanterns hung outside of some temples in Japan on each side of the building's entrance have swastikas each oriented in opposite, symmetrical directions. In the long history of Buddhism, the

30. Chinese incense burner at Buddhist education center, Chinatown, New York.

31. Chinese Buddhist prayer beads.

symbol has been and still is depicted using both orientations. This occurs because in the sutras, the swastika was originally described as right-turning. Very often, those who understand the swastika's meanings and associations prior to WWII are quick to point out that the Buddhist swastika turns in the opposite direction of the Nazi swastika (Hakenkreuz), but that is not always true.

According to J. C. Cooper's *An Illustrated Encyclopedia of Traditional Symbols* (1978), in Chinese the swastika means:

> "The accumulation of lucky signs of Ten Thousand Efficacies." It is an early form of the character *fang* which denoted the four quarters of space and of the earth. Used as a border it depicts the *Wan tzu*, the Ten Thousand Things or Continuities, i.e. infinite duration without beginning or end, infinite renewal of life, perpetuity. It also symbolizes perfection; movement according to the law; longevity; blessing; good augury; good wishes. The blue swastika denotes infinite celestial virtues; the red, infinite sacred virtues of the heart of Buddha; yellow, infinite prosperity; green, infinite virtues in agriculture. The clockwise swastika is *yang*, counter clockwise *yin*.[73]

The two swastikas—clock-wise and counter-clockwise—are used to depict the *yin* and *yang* forces. Whether in Tibet related to Bon or in China related to Taoism, whether right-turning or left-turning, the swastika was an ancient and widespread auspicious symbol of good fortune in Asia, influenced by Buddhism (Figs. 30–33).

32. Korean Buddha Day's lanterns with swastika.

33. Tibetan cloth with four swastikas.

American Buddhism and European Buddhism have developed with the absence of the swastika symbol, though many students in the West learn about the symbol as they study Buddhist teachings and cultures. The spread of Buddhism in the West occurred mostly after World War II, so it was natural to avoid using the swastika there where it was feared it might create the wrong image. Instead of the swastika, the Dharma-wheel and lotus are often used as Buddhist emblems in the West. This approach by Western Buddhists has helped create ignorance in the West about the swastika symbol. In this sense, it is a Buddhist responsibility to educate the misinformed public about the sacred symbol of the swastika, so the larger public can understand that in Asian religious contexts, it has nothing to do with the racism and hatred of Nazism or racist supremacy groups.

TWO

A Universal Symbol

The swastika is one of the world's oldest and most universal symbols, possibly dating to prehistoric times. It is found in ancient ruins all over the globe. It has been used for thousands of years in Eastern religions including Buddhism, Hinduism, and Jainism. Prior to WWII, Native Americans on both the North and South American continents used the symbol extensively. It can be seen on artifacts from ancient Mu, Mayan, Aztec, and Inca civilizations. In Europe it has been discovered in Roman and Greek ruins including Troy. The symbol has also been used in parts of Africa.

Figure 34 is a map taken from *Swastika: The Earliest Known Symbol and Its Migrations* by Thomas Wilson, published in 1894.[74] Wilson's book was the first authoritative text on the history of the swastika written in English. The map shows the swastika's wide geographic distribution, based on Wilson's research. It is clear that the swastika is one of the most circulated religious symbols in human history, appearing since ancient times on five major continents.

Swastika Use in Various Religions

Many world religions, including Buddhism, Hinduism, Jainism, Judaism, Christianity, Islam, and Zoroastrianism, either currently use or have used the swastika at some point during their history as a symbol or at least as a design motif.

As the symbol itself is so ancient, no one knows for sure how exactly it traveled all over the globe in ancient cultures. It can be assumed it was exchanged as cultures interacted with each other via trade and other contact over many millennia. As people interact, naturally ideas

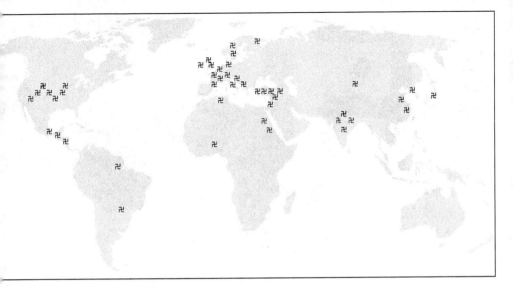

34. Swastika world map based upon Thomas Wilson's book.

are exchanged, along with symbols that represent those ideas. Perhaps because the swastika is such a simple and basic shape, it was easy for different belief systems to adapt the symbol to represent their own ideas.

The swastika's prevalence in different religions also raises the question of why a symbol is needed at all in religion. In order to understand its nature as a symbol, it is useful to consider the 19th-century Christian theologian Paul Tillich's definition of a symbol. According to Tillich, all symbols contain certain fundamental characteristics. As F. W. Dillistone explains in *The Power of Symbols in Religion and Culture*, Tillich makes a clear distinction between symbol and sign.

> Each points beyond itself to something else, but whereas a sign is univocal, arbitrary and replaceable, having no intrinsic relationship with that to which it points, a symbol actually participates in the reality towards which it is directed and which in some degree it represents. It does this not independently but in the power of that to which it points.[75]

Tillich also explains that a symbol "participates in the power of what it symbolizes." It functions to "open up to humans levels of reality which could not be apprehended otherwise."[76]

Tillich says:

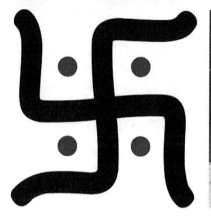

35. Hindu swastika symbol.

36. Harappa seal with swastika, Mohenjo Daro, Indus valley (ca. 2500 B.C.).

> Religious symbols mediate ultimate reality through things, persons, events which, because of their mediating functions, receive the quality of "holy." In the experience of holy places, times, books, words, images, and acts, symbols of the holy reveal something of the "Holy-itself" and produce the experience of holiness in persons and groups.[77]

Although Tillich was a Christian theologian, his definition of symbols corresponds to that which is found in my own tradition of Buddhism as well.

From a Buddhist perspective, all teachings are symbols of greater truth. Symbols, as a visual representation of teachings, are the gateway to understanding the teachings, though they themselves are not the truth itself. Nagarjuna, a 1st-century teacher of Mahayana Buddhism, from which East Asian Buddhism is derived, once said, "Do not mistake the finger pointing to the moon for the moon itself."[78] The finger, or symbol, makes us look in a certain direction and in that direction lies the truth itself. Yet one cannot find that direction without the finger to point us there. This is why symbols are essential in Buddhism and perhaps all religions as well. Without the symbol, one cannot see the truth; one cannot see the truth directly because truth itself is beyond form. But without the form one cannot go anywhere. The teachings can only be understood through some kind of form. A symbol such as the swastika is meant to open up one's thinking. However, because of its desecration and re-signification in the 20th century due to the Nazi appropriation of it, the swastika instead has the effect in the West of shutting down one's thinking.

37. Embossed Square metal plaque of "Lord Shri Ganeshji" with Hindu swastikas.

[1] Hinduism

While Jains and Buddhists have used the swastika symbol for more than 2,000 years, Hindus, possibly the oldest religious community in the East, have been using the swastika for more than 3,000 years and possibly as many as 5,000 years (Fig. 35). The Japanese Buddhist dictionary *Bukkyogo Daijiten*, by the Buddhist scholar Hajime Nakamura, explains that the symbol originates in Hinduism as a symbol of the Indian god Vishnu. Both Jainism and Buddhism originated around the same time in India, in about 500 B.C. The swastika is a common symbol of these major religions, both of which began in India. The swastika, in this sense, is the ancient interfaith symbol of the East.

Excavation sites in Harappa and Mohenjo-Daro in the Indus valley revealed seals with swastika symbols dating back to 2,500 B.C. (Fig. 36). In contrast to Buddhism, the right-turning swastika is generally used in the Hindu tradition, where it is a symbol of auspiciousness, good luck, and blessings. The swastika is identified with Vishnu, as a sun or fire symbol. In Hinduism, the Buddha is considered the ninth of Vishnu's ten incarnations, and is depicted with a swastika sign on his chest. The swastika was also "identified with Shiva and the snake cults of the Naga civilization, originating possibly from the markings on a cobra's hood or the entwined knotting of serpents."[79] Author J. C. Cooper explains that the swastika in Hinduism is "a symbol of the Vedic fire god and divine carpenter, Agni; the fire-sticks, the 'mystic double Arani'; Dyaus, the ancient Aryan sky god, later Indra; also associated with Brahma, Surya, Vishnu, Siva and with Ganesha [Fig. 37] as pathfinder and god of the crossroads."[80]

In Hinduism, Om (or Aum), the swastika and the Sri Chakra Yantra

38. Om (or Aum) and swastika on a Hindu temple in India.

39. Om (or Aum) and swastika on a Hindu book.

are considered the three most revered symbols (Figs. 38, 39).[81] The swastika symbol is used in Hinduism not only for deities but also for worship services and ritual items. There are "Svasti Mantras," referring to the symbol in Vedas, Hindu sacred texts, which are chanted during religious events and worship services. Swastikas are placed on the right and left sides of the entrance door in temples and homes. On special days, rituals commence by writing the swastika symbol. In yoga, the sitting position of legs crossed with feet resting on top of the thighs is called "Svastikasana," because the leg position resembles the shape of the swastika.[82] Because the swastika represents happiness in Hinduism, it is often displayed at festivals, celebrations and joyful ceremonies, such as weddings.

In Hinduism, the four arms of the swastika represent the four directions—East, South, West, and North. The central point of the swastika also represents the navel of Lord Vishnu or Om. It also "represents four-objectives—righteousness, right wealth, right desires and bliss; four stages of life—Student, Married, Contemplative and Detached; the four Vedas—Rig-Veda, Yajur-Veda, Sama-Veda and Atharva-Veda; four Yugas-Satya, Treta, Dwapara and Kali; and many other four-fold divisions."[83]

[2] Jainism

According to *JAINISM—Religions of Compassion and Ecology*, the comprehensive Jain symbol (Fig. 40)[84] "consists of a crescent of the moon, three dots, the swastika or Om, the palm of a hand with the wheel (Chakra) inset, and an outline figure encompassing all symbols. Each individual symbol is also used in Jainism."[85] The swastika in Jainism means "auspiciousness" as it does in Hinduism and Buddhism.

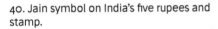

40. Jain symbol on India's five rupees and stamp.

For Jains, the four states of the existence of souls in the world—heaven, human, animal, and hell—are symbolized by the four sides of the swastika. Souls undergo a continuous cycle of birth, suffering, and death in these four states. If one follows religious teachings, it is believed one can be liberated from suffering. The open hand symbol positioned below the swastika symbol signifies non-violence or *Ahimsa*, as it is called in Buddhism. The three circles above it represent the Three Jewels of right belief, right knowledge, and right conduct; the crescent moon represents the state of liberation. The single circle inside of the crescent symbolizes the state of full consciousness, omniscience, or complete liberation. The swastika in Jainism represents the divine force, the Creator of Heaven and Earth.[86] Among the Indian religious traditions, Jainism is most closely associated with *Ahimsa* or non-violence, and its central symbol is the swastika.

Tirthankaras, human beings who have crossed the ocean of birth and rebirth and have thus been released from the bonds of karma, are the central objects of devotion for Jains.[87] The swastika symbol is the emblem of Suparsvanatha, who is the seventh Tirthankara. The wife of the next Tirthankara's father, the Rajput King of Benares, is said to have suffered from leprosy. The disease was cured before the child's birth, so he was given the name *Su* (good) *parsva* (side). His emblem is the swastika symbol.[88]

The swastika is one of the eight special symbols called astamangalas, which appear frequently in Jain art. The *Nandyavarta*, one of the astamangalas, is an extended swastika that represents auspiciousness. In Jain practice, laypersons skilled at drawing will create the eight astamangalas out of grains of rice as part of their temple worship, while others simply draw a swastika in rice on a small table.[89] The swastika symbol appears

41. Jain swastika made with rice.

42. Jain Shrine with swastika (*right*) and *Nandyavarta* (*left*).

on sacred books and in Jain temples as well as in the rice offering ritual mentioned above (Figs. 41, 42).

Currently, each of these three major religions from India has its own primary symbols that the others do not use. Buddhism uses the dharma-wheel (dharma-chakra), Hinduism uses the Om, and Jainism uses the open hand of non-violence. Yet, the swastika is also a common symbol for all three.

Generally speaking, the swastika has a more significant ongoing meaning in the East. But it has also been used extensively in the West, particularly in religions of early civilizations.

[3] Judaism

Swastikas have been discovered at many ancient synagogue excavations. According to *The Universal Jewish Encyclopedia*, "The Swastika appears on various articles excavated in Palestine, on ancient synagogues in Galilee and Syria, and on the Jewish catacombs at the Villa Torlonia in Rome."[90] The swastika was also found at the ancient synagogues of Capernaum, discovered in 1838; Ein Gedi, discovered in 1965; and Maoz Haim, discovered in 1974.

These archeological sites suggest that the swastika was an ancient though forgotten Jewish symbol, or at least a favorite design motif. Scholar Joseph Gutmann says,

> In the synagogue at Capernaum, Galilee, a synagogue which may date from the fourth century C.E., the Magen David is found alongside the pentagram and the swastika, but there

44. Swastika design in mosaic floor of ancient Ein Gedi Synagogue.

43. Swastika pattern at ancient Synagogue of Capernaum.

is no reason to assume that the Magen David or the other signs on the synagogue stone frieze served any but decorative purposes.[91]

Gershom Scholem, another scholar, says,

The hexagram next appears—with a clearly indicated point at its center—only much later among the various ornamental motifs on a frieze that decorates the well-known synagogue of Capernaum [second or third century, Fig. 43]. But the same frieze displays a swastika right next to it, and no one will on that account claim that the swastika might be a Jewish symbol.[92]

Gutmann and Scholem, both writing in the post-WWII era, are perhaps making an effort here to refuse to acknowledge the swastika as a Jewish symbol though its presence at ancient synagogues clearly indicates it was a part of ancient Jewish history.

Among more recent excavation sites, the swastika was found at the synagogue of Ein Gedi in 1965 (Fig. 44).

The indigenous Jewish town of Ein Gedi was an important source of balsam for the Greco-Roman world until its destruction by Byzantine emperor Justinian as part of his persecution of the Jews in his realm. The Synagogue, a street, a Miqwe (Mikveh) and a number of buildings are visible on the site... In 1965, 300 meters northeast of Tel Goren, remains of a mosaic floor were discovered accidently.... In its northern wall, facing Jerusalem, were two openings. The floor was of simple white mosaic with a swastika pattern in black tesserae

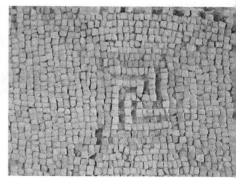

45. Swastika design in mosaic floor of ancient Maoz Haim Synagogue.

in the center. This pattern has been interpreted as a decorative motif or as a good luck symbol.[93]

A 1974 excavation on the Moaz Haim kibbutz, on the border of Jordan, unearthed the remains of three ancient synagogues (Fig. 45).

Originally, it was just a simple structure, but later some Roman basilica-style structures with windows that were traditionally pointed towards Jerusalem were added. The floors were paved with small stones of about 70 different hues depicting Itzhak's sacrifice, the Ark of the Covenant, inscriptions in Hebrew and Aramaic, traditional Jewish symbols, such as the menorah, customary national ornaments, and many different swastikas. Avshalom (the Kibbutz owner) who is 91, has an excellent memory and possesses a detailed historical knowledge of this place, which dates back to 400–600 A.D.... In the next layer of the excavation, they found the 3rd century Jewish settlement named Baala, where Jews had lived for more than 300 years (the settlement of Baala is mentioned in 1 of the 3 parts of the Old Testament).

When asked about how swastikas found their way into a synagogue, Avshalom answered, "All Jewish archeologists that had been working here did not pay any attention to swastikas. People all over the world have been using this ancient symbol of happiness for millennia. This swastika is hundreds of years old. At that time, Hitler was not born yet, how could this fiend be more powerful than the world's history, world's art, and world's culture? I think now it is a right time for all of mankind to put in order some acquired erroneous concepts regarding the swastika symbol."[94]

46. Menorah and swastikas, ancient Umm el Kanatir Synagogue.

There are other ancient examples of swastikas found in Israel. These include a swastika carved together with an image of a menorah at the Umm el Kanatir synagogue which was built in the 6th century A.D. (Fig. 46). The Magden David and menorah are both recognized Jewish symbols. The appearance of the swastika alongside them may suggest that the swastika was also used as a symbol.

[4] Christianity

Although many see the crucifix cross as the central religious symbol of Christianity, it was not formally adopted by the Church until the 6th century. "Of the many forms of the cross, the Swastika is the most ancient."[95] The swastika appears frequently as early as the first and second century as a symbol in catacombs signifying Christ as the power of the world.[96]

According to the *Dent Dictionary of Symbols in Christian Art*, the swastika is "in the art of the catacombs, a cryptic symbol of Christ's power. It comprises four gammas (the third letter of the Greek alphabet) joined together at the foot and so was later interpreted as the Four Evangelists with Christ as their center."[97] Here, Christ can be seen as symbolized as the "Sun of Righteousness," described in the Old Testament: Malachi 4:2. In medieval times the Gammadion, as the swastika was known, was used to symbolize Christ as the cornerstone and also the four Evangelists, with Christ as the center. The four Evangelists Matthew, Mark, Luke, and John represent each gamma. There are various versions of the cross that have been used in Christianity, including the Greek Cross, Tau Cross, Latin Cross, Peter's Cross, the Saltier (X-shaped cross), and the Gammadion.

47. Swastika symbols on an Abbot's Mitre. 8th century, Mitre Cahier, Melanges d'Archelolgie.

48. Swastika symbols on an Abbot's Mitre on a 1922 effigy of Huyshe Wolcott Yeatman, Bishop of Coventry Cathedral, England.

The Dent Dictionary of Symbols in Christian Art further explains that the swastika, "together with the Egyptian key of life was used by the early Christians long before they adopted the cross as the symbol of their religion, and the later cross is absolutely absent in the oldest Christian catacombs of Rome.... A Roman Catholic archeologist suggests that the swastika was the monogram of Jesus, in which Christ's name was spelled Zesus and thus abbreviated into two crossed Z's."[98] It is believed the swastika used by early Christians was adopted from another source and gradually superseded by the Christogram and the cross as the emblem of Christianity.[99]

The catacomb di St. Callisto shows the symbols found on early Roman Catholic tombs: fish; swastika; shepherd with a sacrificed lamb; symbol XP (Chi and Rho, the Greek letters symbolizing Christos); and anchor. The cross is absent.

Even when the crucifix cross became the dominant symbol of Christianity after the 6th century, the swastika and other forms of the cross were still used. One example is an embroidered abbot's mitre from the 8th century.[100] The swastika appears as a motif on abbots' mitres through the early part of the 20th century. It can be found on the 1922 effigy of Huyshe Wolcott Yeatman, Bishop of England's Coventry Cathedral (Figs. 47, 48).[101] The swastika can be found at other cathedrals in Europe including Christ Church Cathedral in Oxford, France's Notre-Dame d'Amiens, and Hereford Cathedral in England, all of which feature swastika designs in their floor tilework (Fig. 49).

The Byzantine swastika, also known as a "gammadion cross" or "crux gammata" is found in medieval churches of the former Byzantine Empire (Figs. 50–53). The swastika's presence at such sites suggests it may have

49. Swastika patterns on the tiles in the choir section of Christ Church Cathedral, Oxford, Oxfordshire, England.

been considered a sacred symbol held in high esteem by the Byzantines, or was at least a popular design motif. The symbol's use in this area can be traced at least as far back as the time of ancient Greece. Swastika symbols can be seen inside the Hagia Sophia Cathedral in Istanbul, Turkey, dedicated in A.D. 360[102] Swastika patterns can also be found on "Sarcofago di Stilicone" in Milano, Italy. It is an Ancient Roman Christian sarcophagus in the 4th century. The Church of Christ Pantocrator, an Eastern Orthodox church built in the late 13th or early 14th century in the eastern Bulgarian town of Nesebar, is designed in the cross-in-square style of the late Byzantine. It is a part of the Ancient Nesebar UNESCO World Heritage site. The church is known for its ornate brick swastika decorative friezes running along its exterior east wall.

Use of the swastika in Bulgaria and other parts of Europe actually predates Christianity. Archaeologists in 2010 unearthed what appears to be the bottom of a 2,500-year old drinking vessel featuring a swastika during excavations of a religious site in Altimir, Bulgaria. This artifact is believed to be Europe's oldest clearly drawn individual swastika.[103] A 10,000-year-old Ice Age ivory bird figurine with a swastika-like geometric design carved into it has been discovered at the Mezine archeological site in Ukraine.[104]

The swastika is found at Ethiopian Orthodox churches in both church architecture and on ritual items such as a priest's staff, used at the Church of St. George in Lalibela, which features a cross made from a combination of swastikas and crosses with a sun symbol at its center (Fig. 54). The combination of all three symbols shows their associations with each other and that the swastika was considered one form of the sacred Christian cross. St. George is one of several churches that were carved

50. Hagia Sophia Cathedral, Istanbul, Turkey.

51. Swastika patterns on an ancient Roman Christian sarcophagus in Milano, Italy (4th century).

52. Swastika friezes running along the east wall of the Church Christ Pantocrator in Bulgaria.

53. Friezes with swastika motifs from Byzantine Egypt.

54. Ethiopian Orthodox Christian cross with swastikas and various cross design windows on the wall of the Beta Medhane Alem Church, Lalibela (Ethiopia, Africa).

whole out of rock during the 12th and 13th centuries in Lalibela. Several of them, including St. Mary's and Church of the Savior of the World, feature swastika-shaped windows and other swastikas in bas-relief and haut-relief.[105]

[5] Islam

Swastika patterns are found in mosque architecture around the world, though their use is not as prevalent in Islam as in other religions (Figs. 55–59). The symbol does not appear to have an importance in modern Islam and it is not well known among scholars what the significance of the symbol was in early Islam.

Islamic culture may have simply adopted the good luck swastika patterns from pre-existing usage in local cultures as Islam spread to different areas throughout the Middle East and Pakistan, Afghanistan, and India. It is documented that the swastika was widespread in Ancient Persia before Islamic settlement. Figure 60 shows the Quadruple ornaments "Ali," "Mohammad," and "Allah" from the Friday Mosque of Isfahan.[106]

There are few mentions of it in scholarship on Islamic symbology. One interpretation for the swastika's symbolic meanings in the context of Islam can be found in J. C. Cooper's *An Illustrated Encyclopedia of Traditional Symbols*, though Cooper does not provide a source for his interpretation. According to Cooper:

> Among Asian Muslims the swastika expresses the four cardinal directions and control of the four seasons by angels, one at each point: West, the Recorder; South, Death; North, Life; East, the Announcer.[107]

The swastika often appears on walls and pillars as a design feature of mosques of the Ottoman Empire, which spanned the 13th–20th centuries. Mughal architecture in India is a distinctive architectural style created by the Mughals during the Mughal Empire from the 16th century to the 18th century. Emperor Akbar (1556–1605) advocated toleration toward the Hindu religion and respect for the culture of the indigenous people of India. The architecture of his reign evolved into an amalgam of both Hindu and Islamic art.

55. Dagger with Arabic inscription with swastika, probably originated in the Islamic Middle East (13th century).

56. Swastika patterns seen on a gate decoration, from the "The Prophet Muhammad Visiting the Heavenly Pavilion of Abraham" (1466).

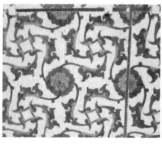

57. Ceramic tile in Turkey, Ottoman Dynasty (1560).

59. Ali's name in tilework Kufic Calligraphy alongside swastikas (Shiite Muslim), Friday Mosque, Yazd, in Iran.

58. Iranian mosque.

60. Quadruple ornaments "Ali," "Mohammad," and "Allah."

61. Main gateway of the tomb of Akbar.

62. Swastika along with Muslim seal at Agra Fort, capital city of Akbar in India.

In Hindu architecture the swastika was not used as a decorative motif but was instead used as an auspicious symbol. The swastika appears as one of many ornamental geometrical designs in Mughal architecture and art. Some scholars, however, believe that the usage of the swastika at certain locations during this period, such as at the entrance of a tomb, could have been used also with a symbolic meaning or as protection from evil spirits (Figs. 61, 62).[108]

[6] Zoroastrianism and other religions

In the Zoroastrian religion of ancient Persia, the swastika represented the revolving sun, the source of life-giving fire and infinite creativity. Some scholars believe that Zoroastrianism, a pre-Christian monotheistic

63. Tash-Khovli Palace column with a swastika at the base.

64. Nkotimsefo Mpua.

65. Ashanti goldweight with swastika, Ghana (13th century).

66. *Left:* Terracotta bowl on the high stand with swastika (4th quarter of 8th century B.C.). *Right:* Terracotta neck-amphora (storage jar) with swastika (560 B.C.).

religion, heavily influenced the development of Judaism, which in turn influenced Christianity and Islam.

The Tash-Khovli (Khauli) Palace of Khiva in the Khorezm region of Uzbekistan has a swastika at the base of a pillar (Fig. 63). Many scholars believe that ancient Khorezm was the birthplace of Zoroastrianism and its prophet Zaratushtra. Archaeological research has linked Zoroastrian doctrine and its cult of fire and natural elements with religious conceptions of primitive Khorezmians. Zoroastrianism spanned three great empires across the Near East—the Akheminid, the Persian, and the Sasakhid—over more than a millennia from the fourth century B.C. to the seventh century A.D. Zoroastrian doctrine can be considered the first world religion. Elements of Zoroastrianism were later absorbed into Christianity, Buddhism, and Islam in the region. It is believed that Judaism incorporated some elements from Zoroastrianism including the sacred symbols of the Star of David, the pentagram, and the swastika during the time of the Babylon captivity.[109]

There are many local religions and cultures existing in the world that use the swastika with their own meanings (Figs. 64, 65). Royal court attendants of the Akan people in Ghana, Africa, wore their hair shaved in a swastika shape called "nkotimsefo mpua" which symbolized loyalty and readiness to serve.[110] Some Akan goldweights have a design of swastika.

Since other Swastika books such as Wilson's *Swastika* discuss swastika symbols in various cultures of the world, I will skip a detailed discussion of cultural aspects. However, when examining the definition of "swastika" in a later chapter, we will encounter the phrase "a Greek cross" to explain the swastika. So I invite you to take a brief look at some examples of gammadion or swastika in ancient Greece. The swastika appeared in Greece, long before Christianity (Fig. 66).

* * *

It is impossible to list here all of the many swastika symbols that appear in both religious and secular uses around the world throughout history. It is clear that the swastika has had a rich and widespread use throughout most of the globe for thousands of years. The swastika is not just any symbol but one of the most common and valued symbols used by human beings throughout human history, culturally, religiously ,and spiritually. It is this broadness that makes it a very common symbol in human culture. It can be said that with the exception of its twisted usage

67. Galaxy.

in the 20th century by the Nazis, the swastika has been the universal symbol of good luck on earth. Its global history over many millennia makes it an all-encompassing symbol that connects beyond culture, beyond time. That broadness recalls the larger galaxy our planet is a smaller part of, the galaxy whose shape actually is the swastika (Fig. 67). Perhaps the swastika is so universal because the swastika *is* the shape of our universe.

The Swastika Symbol in North America

[1] Native American Indians and the "whirl-log"

The swastika has existed as a symbol for Native American Indians since before the arrival of Columbus. The earliest evidence of the swastika in pre-historic America was found in excavations in 1881 at Fains Island and Toco Mounds in Tennessee, at Hopewell Mound, Chillicothe and Ross County in Ohio, and in Poinsett County in Arkansas. Swastika use has been documented among the Kansas, Sac, Pueblo, Navajo, and Pima tribes.[111] An archaeological survey done in the Lower Mississippi Alluvial Valley in the 1940s reported finding swastikas on various native items including jars, bottles, vessels, bowls, and pots.[112]

The swastika has had different meanings depending upon the tribe (Figs. 68–72). Navajo Indians in Arizona, Utah, and New Mexico saw it as sacred symbol for healing and used it solely in their religious ceremonies in the form of sand paintings. Among the Navajos, the swastika is known as the "whirling log" or "that which revolves."

Hopis in northeastern Arizona see the swastika as the center of their

68. Native American quilt with whirling log.

69. Native American craft by Tohono O'odham.

70. Native American basket.

71. Native American accessories.

72. Swastika uniform of Native American basketball team in 1909.

ancestral land, and as a symbol of the four directions of the migration routes of their tribe.[113]

"The Most Misunderstood Mark,"[114] an article by William Manns, describes how "in the pre-war West, the swastika had nothing to do with the Nazis and everything to do with good luck." From 1880 to 1940, the swastika was a popular pattern used in Navajo rugs. Navajo-engraved silver spoons became coveted souvenirs, and one of the most popular motifs was the swastika. The Navajo referred to the swastika as "nohokos" meaning "wishes of well being or blessing on you." The design was widely recognized in popular culture as "Indian good luck." It was adopted by white settlers in the Southwest and spread across the Old West, according to Manns. Cowboys used the swastika along with the four-leaf clover and horseshoe as a good fortune insignia on their holsters and saddles. It was favored by the Miller Brothers of 101 Ranch fame who used the symbol for their letterhead and as an element in many of their Wild West Show posters. The swastika was also the emblem of the Santa Fe Railroad Station until WWII.

In 1940, in response to the rise of Hitler's regime under the swastika flag, the Navajo, Papago, Apache, and Hopi tribes formally banned the swastika symbol from native designs of baskets and blanket weaving, and set afire items that used it. The tribe issued a statement that said: "the above ornament, which has been a symbol of friendship among our forefathers for many centuries, has been desecrated recently by another nation of peoples. Therefore it is resolved that henceforth from this date on and forever more our tribes renounce the use of the emblem commonly known today as the swastika or fylfot on our blankets, baskets, art objects, sand paintings and clothing."[115]

[2] Other Swastikas in the US and Canada before World War II

While the use of the swastika among Native Americans and Wild West cowboys helped spread the symbol between the late 1800s to WWII, archeological discoveries made outside of the Americas during this same period further drove its popularity in the US and Canada as a fashionable lucky charm (Figs. 73–77).

These archeological findings included the 19th-century discovery of ancient Troy and its association with Proto-Indo-Europe, whereby the swastika gained attention in the West as a significant religious symbol of

73. Coca Cola charm (1925).   74. Boy Scout merit badge (early 1900s).

75. US postcard (1907).

distant ancestors. It became a symbol linking European and Indo-Iranian cultures. This popularity peaked in the late 19th and early 20th centuries, and the swastika became known worldwide as a symbol of good luck during this period. The Smithsonian Museum funded research about the swastika by Thomas Wilson that in 1894 resulted in his book *Swastika: The Earliest Known Symbol and Its Migrations*. This book is often cited as the first authoritative work on the worldwide history and usage of the swastika.

The swastika's popularity lasted in the United States until 1930, when the symbol was first appropriated by Hitler as a Nazi insignia and became associated with his Third Reich. Before 1930, the swastika appeared on a diverse array of items including Coca-Cola lucky charms, Boy Scout merit badges, post cards, tiles, poker chips, souvenirs, rugs, clothes, and jewelry—often accompanying the words "good luck." It was also used

76. The Fernie Swastikas (ca. 1922) wore red sweaters with a crooked cross in white, a symbol of good luck until perverted by the Nazis.

77. Silent film, *On Desert Sands* (1915).

as an insignia for sports teams, and as a brand name and logo. The legs of the swastika were said to represent the "four Ls": love, life, light, and luck. The swastika appeared in Hollywood movies about the American West.

A newspaper advertisement from 1917 shows a wide variety of swastika-design jewelry as well as wallets, spoons, and a leather case. The ad proclaims, "To the wearer of the swastika will come from the four winds of Heaven, good luck, long life and prosperity" (Fig. 78). The ad further explains: "the swastika is the oldest cross, and the oldest symbol in the world. Of unknown origin, in frequent use in prehistoric times, it historically first appeared on coins as early as the year 315 B.C. and is at present frequently used by the Indians of the Southwest as an ornament and amulet."

The text of the ad clearly makes a great and immediate effort from its starting point to first link the swastika with Christianity by associating its luck with "heaven" and describing it as a "cross," and secondarily describing its prehistoric universal history and "present" association with American Indians. Reading these sentences, one comes away with a sense of the swastika as primarily part of Christianity but also a symbol that was connected to a larger human history. In the early 20th century, American society was still overwhelmingly

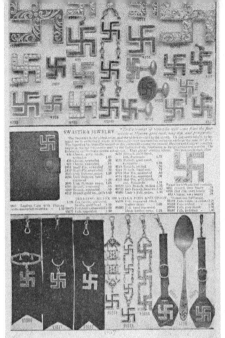

78. Swastika jewelry ad (1917), from the New York Public Library Digital Gallery.

79. Town of "Swastika" in Ontario, Canada.

Christian, and perhaps by promoting this connection to Christianity, any reservations that this was just a superstitious, pagan symbol could be overcome.

The swastika can also be found as a common lucky motif on post cards and greeting cards from the period. A card from the cowcard.com website, which lists more than 60 antique cards with the swastika motif, shows one with a design of a swastika with the Stars and Stripes flag and a message saying, "May our glorious flag and this lucky star guide you and keep you wherever you are."

There are a number of towns in the United States and Canada in which the word "swastika" is part of the name, either for the town itself or for a building. In Black Brook, New York, for example there is a village called "Swastika." One of the main streets through the village is called "Swastika Road."[116] "Swastika Park" is the name of a housing development in Miami, Florida, that dates from the early 1900s. Swastika, Ontario (Fig. 79), in Canada is a small residential community that was known for its gold mining. Townspeople resisted government efforts to change the name during World War II. The name remains today.[117] "Swastika Beach" is in Fish Lake, Minnesota. "Swastika Trail" is a road between Nebraska City, Nebraska, and Keokuk, Iowa. According to the website of the Iowa State Department of Transportation,

80. Subway station wall with swastika, New York City.

81. Library ceiling, Columbia University, New York City.

82. Entrance of Metropolitan Museum of Art, New York City.

When this route was designated, the swastika symbol was recognized for its attributes as a charm or amulet, as a sign of benediction, blessing, long life, good fortune, and good luck. The swastika symbol was popular in the United States prior to 1920, when it was appropriated as a Nazi symbol and later associated with the Third Reich during World War II. The symbol remains visible on numerous historic buildings, including sites that are listed on the National Register of Historic Places. It also appeared on tiles, lampposts, metal valves, tools, surfboards, stock certificates, brand names, place names, medals, commercial tokens, postcards, souvenirs, rugs and clothing.[118]

Swastika patterns from pre-WWII buildings can be found throughout the United States. In New York City swastika borders are visible as an architectural motif at the main branch of the New York Public Library, the Columbia University Library, The Metropolitan Museum of Art, and at some subway stations (Figs. 80–82).

[3] The Swastika as Used by Japanese American Buddhists Before WWII

For Japanese who immigrated to the United States in the late 19th and early 20th centuries, the swastika was not a trendy lucky charm, but rather an important religious symbol that was part of their spiritual and ethnic heritage. Soon after the first wave of Japanese immigrants arrived, so did Japanese Buddhist priests sent over in the late 19th century at the newcomers' request as foreign missionaries from Kyoto's Nishi Hongwan-ji temple to care for their communities. They established the first Japanese Buddhist temple in 1898 in San Francisco. With them came the swastika symbol, which was used extensively in temple architecture, on altars and other ritual items, and on prayer books.

As the population of Japanese immigrant workers grew and spread throughout California and Seattle, and then to Chicago and New York as well, more Nishi Hongwan-ji Jodoshinshu temples and fellowships were established. By the time WWII broke out, there were more than 48 of them throughout the US and Canada unified under an umbrella organization, the Buddhist Missions of North America.

From 1898, for a period of about 40 years, the swastika was used extensively as a sacred Buddhist symbol at these temples. Young Japanese Buddhists organized various religious gatherings, and the swastika is prominent on their banners. Each district had its own banners designed with Buddhist symbols including the swastika. The symbol was used on the facades and roof tiles of temple buildings, and in temple Japanese gardens. It was also used on service books, incense burners, burner tables and other temple objects (Figs. 83–86).

With the rise of Nazism, the previously benign swastika took on seemingly sinister overtones for many Americans. After Pearl Harbor was attacked in 1941, so did the presence of Japanese immigrants, who were suspected of being sympathetic to the Japanese and possible saboteurs. Soon after Pearl Harbor, President Franklin Roosevelt signed Executive Order 9066, which called for the removal of Japanese and Japanese Americans from the West Coast and relocated into internment camps. Some Japanese Americans wondered if the swastika symbol had caused them to be sent to the internment camps because Americans mistakenly thought the symbol meant they had Nazi sympathies.[119] Buddhist temples were shut and their priests were the first group to be rounded up and detained.

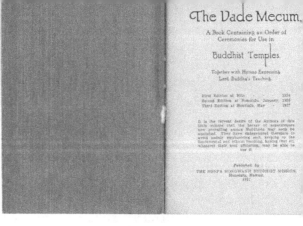

The Vade Mecum.

A Book Containing an Order of Ceremonies for Use in

Buddhist Temples.

Together with Hymns Expressing Lord Buddha's Teaching.

First Edition at Hilo   1924
Second Edition at Honolulu, January   1926
Third Edition at Honolulu, May   1927

83. Front cover with swastika and interior of service book published by the Honpa Hongwanji Buddhist Mission, Honolulu, Hawaii, in 1927.

84. *Left*: Bay District Young Women's Buddhist Association banner with swastika (1934). *Right*: Northern California District manner with swastika, California Young Buddhist League Conference in Fresno (April 1938).

85. Buddha's Birthday (Hanamatsuri) flower shrine with flower-swastika on front roof in Fresno, California (1937).

86. Swastika on the center entrance facade of the Marysville Buddhist Church, California (1935).

Japanese immigrants In California and other Western states had long faced discrimination even before the war. This intensified after Japan's alliance with Germany in 1940 and the Pearl Harbor attack the following year. Two men, 65-year-old Jungo Kino and 43-year-old Frank Yoshioka were murdered in Stockton, California, in early 1941, but the case was unsolved. Incidents of violence by whites against those of Japanese descent were often quickly dismissed in court. Japanese Buddhist temples were frequently attacked. Scholar Duncan Ryuken Williams describes in *Issei Buddhism in the Americas* a wartime incident in California:

> What would today be called a "hate crime" were directed against Buddhists, such as an incident in which local white boys took their shotguns to the Fresno Buddhist Temple and used the front entrance of the building for target practice. Their potshots were particularly aimed at the ancient Buddhist symbol called manji, which represented an aerial view of a stupa and which adorns many Buddhist temples around the world....[120]

Once the war broke out, Japanese American Buddhists saw no other choice than to stop using the swastika symbol, as Tetsuden Kashima explains in *Buddhism in America:*

> The racist hysteria that followed the Japanese bombing of Pearl Harbor and pending internment persuaded even the most tradition-conscious Buddhists that they no longer could afford to retain the reverse swastika as a religious emblem in

87. Japanese garden surrounded by swastika border stones at the Fresno Buddhist Church.

their architecture, despite its long tradition as an Indian symbol for Buddhism and its extensive use in American Buddhist temples. Public perceptions of its meaning immediately were transformed with the advent of war. The reverse swastika was misinterpreted as a sign of loyalty to the Axis powers, providing tangible "evidence" to confirm existing prejudices about the suspect status of people of Japanese descent in America. So, Buddhists reluctantly removed these signs from their architecture and related material culture in the closing days before internment. In the post-war period they substituted more benign symbols, such as lotuses and eight-spoked wheels, in architectural ornamentation.[121]

Josephine Nock-Hee Park explains the difficult situation of Buddhists in that era:

After Pearl Harbor, Buddhist priests were in the first group rounded up and incarcerated, and the Nazi resignification of the Buddhist symbol of the swastika dramatically symbolizes the grave liability of being a Buddhist in this era."[122]

The war had transformed the swastika into not just a symbol of anti-Semitism, but anti-Japanese sentiment that lasted even after the war was over, as Lawson Inaba describes:

We moved to Sonoma County in 1946 to try our hands at chicken faming. Tommy was in the second grade. The effects of internment lasted for a long time. For example, he felt pain and confusion when he saw a swastika in a classmate's home and was taunted with anti-Japanese and anti-Semitic insults.

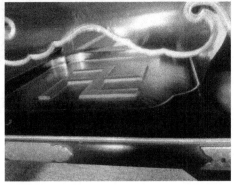

88. Incense burner table with swastika at the Fresno Buddhist Church.

He knew this was wrong, yet he questioned whether he should confront his friend or "keep his mouth shut."[123]

During the war and in the years immediately after the war, rather than confront the discrimination and challenge it, Japanese American Buddhists for the most part were silent and instead sought to erase the marks of differentness from mainstream America that had made them a target. In 1944 a group of ministers and lay leaders gathered at the Topaz internment camp and officially changed the name of the Buddhist Missions of North America (BMNA) to the Buddhist Churches of America (BCA). Describing their religious centers as "churches" allowed them to blend less conspicuously into mainstream predominantly Christian American society. Buddhists, especially clergy, generally faced a much more difficult internment experience than their Christian counterparts, although they were allowed to conduct services and other rituals and practice their faith while in camp. Many of the older Buddhist priests were sent to the Tule Lake camp, considered the harshest of all camps, where those who had refused to sign a loyalty oath declaring their loyalty to the United States were held.

The BCA completely stopped using the swastika symbol after World War II, switching instead to the more benign dharma wheel and the Nishi Hongwan-ji weeping wisteria crest as its official emblems. The symbol still survives, however, on pre-war altar furniture still used at some BCA temples, and on some architectural details such as the remaining swastika-shaped garden paving stones at the Fresno Buddhist Church (Figs. 87, 88). It can still be seen at the Japanese American National Museum in LA, where several wooden pews with carved swastikas can

89. An original pew (*left*) and stair railings (*right*) with swastika design used at Nishi Hongwan-ji Betsuin Buddhist temple in Los Angeles before WWII.

be seen along with wrought iron railings with a swastika design, leftovers from the building's original function as the Nishi Hongwan-ji Betsuin Buddhist temple (Fig. 89).[124] The Museum's archives hold many historic photos and materials pertaining to the history of the BMNA and BCA temples.

Like American Indians, for whom the swastika had also been a sacred symbol that was an important part of their culture, faced with its abrupt resignification as an emblem of America's enemy, Japanese Americans chose simply to abandon it rather than challenge its desecration. This was seen as necessary. Both American Indians and Japanese Americans were at different times already considered enemies of the United States, even when they were born here, and therefore had a greater historical burden placed upon them to prove they were in fact loyal Americans.

But perhaps more than any other persona in WWII, it was Adolf Hitler who was seen as the personification of the evil enemy that America was fighting against. Therefore it was "his" emblem that became the symbol of that evil. Hitler's appropriation of the swastika marked a dramatic and complete resignification in the eyes of the Western world of what for thousands of years previous was instead a symbol of all that was good. How could such a thing occur?

THREE

Hitler's Flag

I myself always came out for the retention of the old colors, not only because as a soldier they are to me the holiest thing I know, but because also in their esthetic effect they are by far the most compatible with my feeling. Nevertheless, I was obliged to reject without exception the numerous designs which poured in from the circles of the young movement, and which for the most part had drawn the swastika into the old flag. I myself—as Leader—did not want to come out publicly at once with my own design, since after all it was possible that another should produce one just as good or perhaps even better. Actually, a dentist from Starnberg did deliver a design that was not bad at all, and, incidentally, was quite close to my own, having only the one fault that a Swastika with curved legs was composed into a white disk.

Mein Kampf[125]

Design of the Hook-Cross

The "old colors" that Hitler refers to were the black, red, and white of the German Republic national flag used from 1871 until Germany's defeat in 1918. To Hitler, these colors clearly recalled the glory days of the Empire, prior to the humiliation of the Weimar Republic, whose flag colors were red, black, and gold. But Hitler was creating a new movement rather than restoring an old one, and therefore needed a new design to represent its own philosophy, character, and vision for Germany's new future. These colors were not new, but had appeared on flags going back to the early days of the Hanseatic League that existed from the 13th to the 17th century. For the German empire, red, white, and black were combinations of the colors of Prussia (black and white) and the Hanseatic colors (red and white). They also symbolized the Margraviate of Brandenburg, which preceded the Kingdom of Prussia.[126] Hitler, while keeping these old colors, reassigned them new meanings. Similar to what he did with the ancient swastika symbol, he took that which preexisted and already was somewhat familiar, and gave it a whole new meaning from his own imagination and detached from its origins.

In *Mein Kampf*, Hitler explains:

> As National Socialists, we see our program in our flag. In red we see the social idea of the movement, in white the nationalistic idea, in the Swastika the mission of the struggle for the victory of the Aryan man, and, by the same token, the victory of the idea of creative work, which as such always has been and always will be anti-Semitic.[127]

The new flag needed to be something that could appeal to the masses. Hitler said that in the early days of the Nazi party,

> ... The movement possessed no party insignia and no party flag. The absence of such symbols not only had momentary disadvantages, but was intolerable for the future.... For the new flag had to be equally a symbol of our own struggle, since in the other hand it was expected also to be highly effective as a poster. Anyone who has to concern himself much with the masses will recognize these apparent trifles to be very important matters. An effective insignia can in hundreds of thousands of cases give the first impetus toward interest in a movement.[128]

The flag would be the center of his propaganda, something that through one powerful image could reflect the essence of the movement. With his own artistic background, Hitler was undoubtedly conscious of the importance of the visual impact of a salient flag design.

> What importance must be attributed to such a symbol from the psychological point of view I had even in my youth more than one occasion to recognize and also emotionally to understand. Then, after the War, I experienced a mass demonstration of Marxists in front of the Royal Palace and the Lustgarten. A sea of red flags, red scarves and red flowers gave to this demonstration, in which an estimated hundred

and twenty thousand persons took part, an aspect that was gigantic from the purely external point of view. I myself could feel and understand how easily the man of the people succumbs to the suggestive magic of a spectacle so grandiose in effect.[129]

Hitler took great pride in the final new flag of Nazi Germany:

In midsummer of 1920 the new flag came before the public for the first time. It was excellently suited to our new movement. It was young and new, like the movement itself. No one had seen it before; it had the effect of a burning torch.[130]

There is evidence from the Nazi Party Central Archives of Hitler's interest in using the swastika as an emblem possibly as early as before 1905, when he was still a student. It is believed that either during this time, or in the period between 1905 and 1913 that Hitler designed a book cover for a book he was writing titled *The Germanic Revolution.* The design of the cover shows the Hakenkreuz swastika in the same form as that of the National-Socialist Party after 1920.[131]

Jorg Lanz von Liebenfels (1874–1954), an Austrian journalist and former Catholic monk, founded the Order of the New Templars, *"Ordo novi templi"* in 1907. The Templars were an esoteric and anti-Semitic organization dedicated to promoting Aryan racial dominance over "lower" races. He pledged to violently counter the socialistic class struggle with a race struggle "to the hilt of the castration knife."[132] During a Christmas Day celebration at Burg Werfen-stein in 1907, Lanz raised two flags, one of which carried a design of an untilted red swastika, surrounded by four blue fleurs-de-lis (heraldic seals) on a golden background.[133] Lanz in that moment became the first person to use the swastika as a symbol for Aryans and anti-Semitism (Fig. 90). Lanz founded the magazine *Ostara* in 1905, based upon anti-Semitic and volkisch theories, which young Hitler enjoyed reading. *Ostara* was a gateway for Hitler to learn about anti-Semitism and Aryan race theories. Hitler reportedly even visited Lanz to obtain missing copies of *Ostara* to complete his own collection of all editions of the magazine. Hitler therefore must have been familiar with Lanz's swastika flag.

In 1908, Guido von List (1848–1919), the German/Austrian occultist, published the *Secret of the Runes*, which is considered by scholars as a

90. Swastika flag by Jorg Lanz von Liebenfelt (1907).

Guido von List
Das Geheimnis
der Runen

91. Cover page of the *Secret of the Runes* (1908).

pioneering work in the study of runes. List's first German edition had a symbol on the front cover comprised of a swastika surrounded by 18 runes (Fig. 91). It is more sharply angled than the Nazi swastika. In the German version, List refers to the ᛤ symbol as "Fyrfos," or "Hakenkreuz."[134]

The swastika also was used by a German right wing anti-Semitic group, the Germanenorden (or "Order of Teutons") founded by Theodor Fritsch in 1912, which had a curved version on a cross as its emblem.[135] Wandervogel, a nationalistic German youth movement also used the swastika as an insignia from 1914. Wandervogel influenced the development of both the National Socialists and the Hitler Youth.

Hitler's own words in *Mein Kampf*, quoted above, show that Hitler already had the design in his head when Dr. Friedrich Krohn, a dentist from Starnberg and a prominent member of the German Worker's Party and Nationalist-Socialist Party, suggested using a swastika with curved legs on the flag. Doctor Krohn's design was probably similar to the symbol of the Thule Society (or *Thule-Gesellschaft*) of which Dr. Krohn was a member. The Thule Society was a German occult group whose goal was to recreate what they believed was a race of Aryan supermen with psychic powers who allegedly inhabited the lost city of Atlantis, and whose power was lost due to generations of race mixing. Their logo included a swastika design similar to that which Hitler described Dr. Krohn submitting. Shown here are the Thule Society logo (Fig. 92) and Dr. Krohn's design (Fig. 93). Figure 93 is based on Hitler's description of Dr. Krohn's design in *Mein Kampf*.

Hitler did not explain why he chose the right-turning swastika instead of the left-turning one, or why he tilted the swastika 45 degrees (Fig. 94). There is no documented evidence of why he chose to tilt it, though

92. Thule Society logo.

93. How Dr. Krohn's design may have looked.

94. Nazi emblem (1923).

speculation and guesses abound. Some writers have theorized that tilting the symbol at this angle suggests the symbol of the SS, **⚡⚡** , which was said to be based on the Nordic Sig-rune, also called the victory rune. In this way, the Hakenkreuz swastika can be seen as two crossed runes **⚡⚡**.

The Nordic symbol runes appear as the sign for an s-sound and an e-sound.[136] If so, **⚡** may be seen as "S" of the German word for victory, Sieg. Hitler often used this word, most notably the **⚡** rune was the symbol of German victory.

The word "Sieg" is used twice in Hitler's explanation of the meaning of the Hakenkreuz swastika. Hitler says,

> im Hakenkreuz die Mission des Kampfes für den Sieg des arischen Menschen und zugleich mit ihm auch den Sieg des Gedankens der schaffenden Arbeit, die selbst ewig antisemi-tisch war und antisemitisch sein wird.[137]

The Hakenkreuz swastika may possibly be interpreted as representing the "Sieg" (victory) of the Aryan people and the "Sieg " (victory) of anti-Semitism, though Hitler himself did not actually say that, so this is speculation.

The 45-degree angle version is the standard form of the Hakenkreuz. Swastika symbols normally are not tilted, though both left turning and right turning swastikas do exist. The 45-degree tilt is a distinguishing feature of the Hakenkreuz, differentiating it from swastikas in general.

卐 , 卍 = Swastika   **卐** = Hakenkreuz

95. Elephant with swastika by the Carlsberg brewery gate.

96. "Swastika" Laundry, Dublin, Ireland.

Hitler and the Eastern Swastika: Swastika Usage in 19th- and 20th-Century Europe

Swastika symbols could be seen all over the Europe when Adolf Hitler was growing up. Hitler himself was an artist who was interested in design motifs, and he therefore would have encountered and noticed the swastika many times.

Heinrich Schliemann, a German businessman and archeologist, discovered many swastika motifs when excavating the ruins of Troy in the late 19th century. Schliemann concluded after consultations with two leading Sanskrit scholars, Emile Burnouf and Max Muller, that the swastika was a Proto-Indo-European symbol. These exciting archeological findings gained much international attention and put the swastika in the spotlight as an "exceedingly significant religious symbol of our ancient ancestors,"[138] in the words of Schliemann. This attention led to the popularization in the early 20th century of the swastika as the worldwide symbol of good luck.

The swastika was used in Europe in the early 20th century as a sign of power and energy. In Sweden, the hokkors (or hook cross, the Swedish word for the symbol) was often used on maps to indicate the location of a power plant. The Swedish electricity company ASEA used a swastika in its logo until the beginning of the 1930s, when it was discontinued because of its Nazi associations. In Denmark, in the first part of the 20th century, the Danish brewery Carlsberg used a swastika as its logo, and on one of the elephant statues by the brewery's gate (Fig. 95). The Swastika Laundry in Dublin, Ireland, used a swastika logo from its establishment

97. Finnish air force plane and its flag.

in 1912 (Fig. 96). Swastikas were used in the insignia of Finland's Air Force in 1918 (Fig. 97).[139]

In Latvia, the swastika was a popular folk symbol dating from the Bronze Age, considered to have protective qualities and often woven into knitwear and other textiles. Known as a "Thunder Cross" or a "Fire Cross," it was used as the emblem of the country's air force and some military units after their independence following World War I until the 1930s. The Anglo-Indian author Rudyard Kipling placed the swastika above his signature on covers and flyleaves of several of his works until the Nazis adopted it.

In the mid-19th century when it was discovered that Buddhists were using the swastika as a symbol of the Buddha, many Christians welcomed the swastika with a prophetic meaning, as a symbol of Christ. William T. Parker says,

> Significance of the swastika is to be accounted for as a great fact or truth divinely communicated in the earliest times as prophetic of the coming of the Agnus Dei, the Light of the World and the Saviour of Mankind ... Every swastika conceals the sign of the cross, and as the books of the Bible are prophetic of the coming of our Lord so this symbol is prophetic of the coming of the Founder of Christianity. It is one of the great religious symbols of the world. It has been revered all over Europe and Asia. It is one of the oldest things in history, and there is scarcely a land in whose ruined temples it is not found.[140]

Did Hitler know of the Eastern swastika? Hitler was born in 1889, during a time when the swastika was well-known and popularized in Germany and other parts of the West. He would have likely encountered it as he grew up in late 19th century, early 20th century Germany. The work of several prominent German scholars including Heinrich Schliemann and Max Muller were driving forces in shining a spotlight in the West on the ancient swastika symbol. The swastika was present around him in various contexts from these scholarly works where it was noted as a religious symbol—although a somewhat misunderstood one—and design motif, to its popular usage as a good-luck symbol. Hitler was also interested in art and architecture and would have also probably noticed its prominent decorative use as well. Therefore it is not surprising that it would have caught his attention and later found its way into the fascist propaganda machine he was creating.

Hitler was certainly aware of the Eastern swastika and its history as an ancient Eastern symbol of the sun, as well as its use in India and Japan. Hitler described the symbol in an anti-Semitic speech given in Munich in August 1920 that marked the debut of the new flag of the National Socialists. According to *Mein Kampf*, this was the earliest version of the Hakenkreuz flag. Hitler saw the symbol as a type of cross, rather than an exotic symbol with a similar appearance. Rather than using the word "swastika" which Muller and others used, during the speech Hitler instead repeatedly referred to the symbol as a Hakenkreuz, or just a "kreuz" (cross). This appears to be Hitler's first known use of the word "Hakenkreuz":

> If this power could not find its full expression in the high North, it became apparent when the ice shackles fell and man turned south to the happier, freer nature. We know that all these northern peoples had one symbol in common—the symbol of the Sun. They created cults of Light and they've created the symbols of the tools for making fire—the drill and the cross. You will find this cross as a Hakenkreuz as far as India and Japan, carved in the temple pillars. It is the Hakenkreuz, which was once a sign of established communities of Aryan Culture.

> *Wir wissen, daß allen diesen Menschen ein Zeichen gemeinsam blieb: das Zeichen der Sonne. Alle ihre Kulte bauen sie auf Licht, und sie finden das Zeichen, das Werkzeug der Feuererzeugung, den Quirl, das Kreuz. Sie finden dieses Kreuz als Hakenkreuz nicht nur hier, sondern genau so in*

Indien und Japan in den Tempelpfosten eingemeißelt. Es ist das Hakenkreuz der einst von arischer Kultur gegründeten Gemeinwesen.[141]

Based upon Hitler's stated knowledge about the swastika symbol, we can say that his flag design was not created by accident, his symbol not randomly chosen, but rather was quite carefully selected and constructed with particular significance and meaning.

FOUR

Hitler's First Meaning of "Hakenkreuz": Aryan

In the Hakenkreuz [we see] ... the mission of the struggle for the victory of the Aryan man, and, by the same token, the victory of ... the idea of creative work, which as such always has been and always will be anti-Semitic.

Mein Kampf

Meaning of "Aryan"

Hitler clearly states here that his swastika emblem, which he called the Hakenkreuz, represents two meanings, one the victory of "Aryan" man, and two, the victory of "anti-Semitism" in all creative work. Hitler did not choose the Hakenkreuz accidentally, and assigned these specific two meanings to the symbol.

By understanding Hitler's assigned meanings of the symbol, we can understand the relationship between Hitler's Hakenkreuz and the Eastern swastika. As seen in the first part of the quote above, Hitler saw the Hakenkreuz as representing the victory of the imagined Aryan race.

Hitler's association of the swastika symbol with the so-called Aryans suggests that he already knew about the history of the swastika and probably had already learned details about its meanings in Eastern cultures. Hitler adapted many popular culture symbols and ideologies at that time, such as rune symbols, Eastern symbols, Darwin's evolutionary theory, Nietzsche's philosophy and Wagner's art and philosophy. He spent five years in Vienna, Austria, which was then the center of excitement and modernization in Europe. He was influenced by art, architecture, music, philosophy, and politics. In the process, he created his own constructs including the Hakenkreuz swastika as well as a new meaning of the word "Aryan."

The word "Aryan" comes from the Sanskrit word "ārya," meaning "noble." In Buddhism and other Eastern traditions, a noble man is a man of happiness, peace, and well-being. *Webster's New World Dictionary of American Language* (Second Edition, 1984), defines the word "Aryan" as:

> Ar·y·an *adj.* [Sans *ārya*, noble, lord (used as tribal name to distinguish from indigenous races), whence Avestan *airya-nam*, IRAN; akin to Gr. *aristos* best]

A New English Dictionary on Historical Principles, by Sir James Murray in 1884, explains the etymology of the term:

> Ar·y·an, Arian *a.* and *sb.* [f. Sanskrit *ārya*, in the later language 'noble, of good family,' but apparently in earlier use a national name 'comprising the worshippers of the gods of the Brahmans' (Max Muller); cf. Zend *ariya* 'venerable,' also a national name ...]

Aryan in the original Sanskrit, is not a category of race or ethnicity at all, but instead describes the qualities of an individual in terms of how he or she acts and lives. It describes one's behavior, not bloodline. The concept of "Aryan" is defined incorrectly in the above entries because it mistakenly associates racial identity with the term. Western scholars as well as Hitler used it to name a race, but that race was imaginary. During the 19th century, Western archeological findings in India revealed ancient advanced cultures. Scholars, including linguist Max Muller and archeologist Heinrich Schliemann, operating under the colonial biases of the era, propagated an assumed, imagined, and unsubstantiated claim that the sophistication of these native non-white cultures was in fact due to a superior white race who invaded, bringing with them advanced culture which then took over more primitive cultures of native dark-skinned peoples.

Ārya in Buddhism

The word *ārya* is a key term in Buddhism, and is used frequently, more so than in Hinduism and Jainism. When studying Buddhism, one first learns the teachings of the *ārya-satya*, the "Four Noble Truths,"[142] as well as the *ārya-ashtangika-marga*, the "Eightfold Noble Paths." Buddhists are called *ārya-samgha*, or *ārya-gana*, meaning a gathering of noble people. A *Ārya-pudgala* is a noble person, an enlightened individual.

These usages show that "Aryan" is inaccurate to use as a name of a race or ethnic group, as it simply means one who practices the noble path of Enlightenment. An individual is noble because of their practice or life style, their behavior, and their actions. "Arya" is not something one can be born with, but rather something one becomes through practice of the Arya Dharma, the Buddha's teachings, a practice which is open to anyone.

In the *Great Forty Sutra* which appears in the Pali Canon, the Buddha explains the cultivation of the Eightfold Noble Paths: right view, right thoughts, right speech, right action, right livelihood, right effort, and right mindfulness. Many Buddhist sutras were written in the Pali language, which is a relative of Sanskrit. The Sanskrit word *ārya* in Pali is *ariya* or *ariyo*. The Sanskrit *ārya-satya* is *ariya-sacca* in Pali; *Ārya-pudgala* is *ariya-puggala*. Here is part of the sutra:

> *Katamo ca bhikkhave, **ariyo** sammāsamādhi saupaniso saparikkhāro, seyyathīdaṃ: sammādiṭṭhi sammāsaṅkappo sammāvācā sammākammanto sammāājīvo sammāvāyāmo sammāsati. Yā kho bhikkhave, imehi sattaha'ṅgehi1 cittassa ekaggatā parikkhatā ayaṃ vuccati bhikkhave, **ariyo** sammāsamādhi saupaniso itipi, saparikkhāro itipi.*[143]

Now what, monks, is **noble** right concentration with its supports and requisite conditions? Any singleness of mind equipped with these seven factors—right view, right thoughts, right speech, right action, right livelihood, right effort, and right mindfulness—is called **noble** right concentration with its supports and requisite conditions....[144]

> *Katamā ca bhikkhave, sammādiṭṭhi **ariyā** anāsavā lokuttarā maggaṅgā: yā kho bhikkhave, **ariya**cittassa anāsavacittassa **ariya**maggasamaṅgino **ariya**maggaṃ bhāvayato paññā paññindriyaṃ paññābalaṃ dhammavicayasambojjhaṅgo sammādiṭṭhi maggaṅgaṃ ayaṃ vuccati bhikkhave, sammādiṭṭhi **ariyā** anāsavā lokuttarā maggaṅgā.*

And, monks, what is the right view that is **noble**, without passions, transcendent, a partial path? Monks, those with the **noble** mind and the mind without passions, investigators of **noble** path, and practitioners of **noble** path gain the roots of Wisdom, the power of Wisdom, and the analytical ability to understand the truth. They are fully possessed of the path. Monks, this is the right view that is **noble**, without passions, transcendent, a partial path....[145]

The *Dhammapada* is a collection of the teachings of the Buddha expressed in simple verses. It is well known for its usage of the term "Ārya" (ariya).[146] Part of the Four Noble Truths described in the *Dhammapada* reads: "Those who take refuge in the three treasures (Buddha, Dharma, and Sangha) are called Buddhists. All Buddhists are the ones who see the Aryan teachings."

*Yo ca buddhanca dhammanca samghanca saranam gato cattari **ariya**saccani sammappannaya passati. Dukkham dukkhasamuppadam dukkhassa ca atikkamam **ariyam** catthangikam maggam dukkhupasamagaminam.*

> One, who takes refuge in the Buddha, the Dharma and the Sangha, sees with ... the Four **Noble** Truths, viz., Dukkha (suffering), the Cause of Dukkha, the Cessation of Dukkha, and the **Noble** Path of Eight Constituents which leads to the Cessation of Dukkha.[147]

In the following three parts of the *Dhammapada* the term "Āryan"'is used as another name of the Buddha, who became a noble being by realizing the noble truth, the dharma, beyond birth-and-death through mindfulness.

*Appamado amatapadam pamado maccuno padam appamatta na miyanti ye pamatta yatha mata. Evam visesato natva appamadamhi pandita appamade pamodanti **ariya**nam gocare rata.*

> Mindfulness is the way to the deathless (nirvana); unmindfulness is the way to death. Those who are mindful do not die; those who are not mindful are as if already dead. Fully comprehending this, the wise, who are mindful, rejoice in being mindful and find delight in the domain of the **Noble** Ones (Ariyas).[148]

*Dhammapiti sukham seti vippasannena cetasa **ariyappavedite**
dhamme sada ramati pandito.*

He who drinks in the Dharma lives happily with a serene
mind; the wise man always takes delight in the Dharma
expounded by the **Noble** Ones (Ariyas).[149]

*Yo sasanam arahatam **ariyanam** dhammajivinam patikkosati
dummedho ditthim nissaya papikam phalani katthakasseva
attaghataya phallati.*

The foolish man who, on account of his wrong views, scorns
the teaching of homage-worthy **Noble** Ones (Ariyas) who live
according to the Dharma is like the bamboo which bears fruit
for its own destruction.[150]

*So karohi dipamattano khippam vayama pandito bhava
niddhantamalo anangano dibbam **ariyabhumim** upehisi.*

Make a firm support for yourself; hasten to strive hard, and be
wise. Having removed impurities and being free from moral
defilements you shall enter the abodes of the **Ariyas** (i.e.,
Suddhavasa brahma realm).[151]

In the following section, the Buddha clearly explains who is and
who isn't Aryan. Under this definition, Hitler and Nazi Germany, which
brought about the murder of millions of human beings, were clearly *not*
Aryan, and were the complete opposite of the actual Buddhist definition
of the word.

*Na tena **ariyo** hoti yena panani himsati ahimsa sabbapapnam
"**ariyo**" ti pavuccati.*

He who harms living beings is, for that reason, not an **ariya** (a
noble One); he who does not harm any living being is called
an **ariya**.[152]

The auspicious sign of the swastika appears on the heart of the Buddha who fulfilled the Aryan (noble) paths with the Aryan (noble) mind
of wisdom, compassion, and *Ahimsa* (no harming). Therefore, the swastika of auspiciousness, good luck, and peace belongs to the Aryan person (noble person). Birth, blood, and race do not make people noble,
but instead their actions make them noble. Hitler's incorrect usages and

resignification of both the swastika and the term Aryan disgraced and damaged both badly. Together with the swastika, the meanings of the Sanskrit word "Ārya" and its derivative "Aryan" also need to be corrected in their misperception in the West.

The Western Concept of What an Aryan Is

In Hitler's time, the European concept of the meaning of the term "Aryan" was very much related to the development of language theory and the discovery of the Sanskrit language in India by the English during the British occupation of India. What we now call the "Proto-Indo-European Language," was also then known as the "Aryan Language."

[1] Discovery of the Sanskrit Language

European scholarship of Sanskrit done in the late 18th century is regarded as responsible for the discovery of the Indo-European language family. It was an exciting discovery of an ancient Asian language that surprised scholars with its elegance. When the English philologist Sir William Jones encountered the Sanskrit language he admiringly said:

> The Sanscrit language, whatever be its antiquity, is of a wonderful structure; more perfect than the *Greek*, more copious than the *Latin*, and more exquisitely refined than either, yet bearing to both of them a stronger affinity, both in the roots of verbs and the forms of grammar, than could possibly have been produced by accident; so strong indeed, that no philologer could examine them all three, without believing them to have sprung from some common source, which, perhaps, no longer exists; there is a similar reason, though not quite so forcible, for supposing that both the *Gothic* and the *Celtic*, though blended with a very different idiom, had the same origin with the *Sanscrit*; and the old *Persian* might be added to the same family.[153]

But the discovery posed a vexing question for European scholars: why did the great language of Sanskrit "more perfect than Greek and more copious than the Latin" exist in India, and not in Europe? It was then that the idea of an Aryan language family came alive. Max Muller, an Anglo-German philologist and Orientalist, first introduced the theory. His *A History of Ancient Sanskrit Literature* was written in 1859, seventy years after Sir William Jones initiated the study of Sanskrit philology. Muller further introduced the connection between the theory of an Aryan language family, Aryan nations, and an Aryan race. He wrote,

> Although the Brahmans of India belong to the same family, the Aryan or Indo-European family, which civilised the whole world of Europe, the two great branches of that primitive race were kept asunder for centuries after their first separation. The main stream of the Aryan nations has always flowed towards the northwest...[154]

Muller's theory of a connection between an Aryan language, race, and nations, he explained, was based on comparative philology. This definition of "Aryan," although Muller later claimed only meant those who speak Aryan language[155] according to the above quotation, clearly refers to a race that "civilized the whole world." It presents the image that those who speak the Aryan language are a superior race. Muller was responsible for popularizing this notion of an Aryan race from the mid-19th century onward, using the term "Aryan" to replace the term "Indo-European."[156] Muller's ideas were influential among other scholars.

Sir Charles Lyell (1797–1875) in his *The Geological Evidences of the Antiquity of Man*, Chapter 23 "Origin of Development of Language and Species Compared" said:

> The supposed existence, at a remote and unknown period, of a language conventionally called the Aryan, has of late years been a favourite subject of speculation among German philologists, and Professor Max Muller has given us lately the most improved version of this theory, and has set forth the various facts and arguments by which it may be defended, with his usual perspicuity and eloquence.[157]

Some however, expressed skepticism. John Crawfurd, in his *Notes on the Antiquity of Man*, warned that Aryan language theory was only a hypothesis without any concrete proof of existence. He said:

> "Sir Charles Lyell has adopted what has been called the Aryan theory of language, and fancies that he finds in it an

illustration of the hypothesis of the transmutation of species by natural selection. The Aryan or Indo-European theory, which has its origin and its chief supporters in Germany, is briefly as follows ... A language which theorists have been pleased to call Aryan is the presumed source of the many languages referred to. But the Aryan is but a language of the imagination, of the existence of which no proof ever has been or can ever be adduced ... The Aryan theory proceeds on the principle that all language are to be traced to a certain residuum called "roots."[158]

Muller's Aryan language hypothesis contributed to another popular "historical" theory, that of an invasion by a northern nomadic light-skinned Indo-European "Aryan" race or tribe from Central Asia around 1500–1000 B.C. which allegedly destroyed the Harappa Civilization and established Aryan or Vedic culture in India. Recent scholars including the renowned archeologist B.B. Lal, challenge Aryan invasion theory, which had been largely accepted in the West, as a baseless story.[159] Lal points out that no literary or archaeological records of India support the hypothesis of an invasion by a light skinned "Aryan" tribe. Modern genetics also do not support the hypothesis. A major genetic study published in 2011 demonstrated that there was no such Aryan/Dravidian divide or invasion from the north.[160] Many contemporary scholars now believe that it was a Eurocentric myth invented to explain the existence of the Sanskrit language in India.

[2] The Swastika as an Aryan Symbol

In Germany, Aryan invasion theory became popular in the 19th century. Hitler was not the first to associate the swastika symbol with the so-called Aryan race. From the mid-1870s, new archaeological discoveries and modern occultism both spurred the development of the Aryan myth by identifying the swastika as a racial symbol.

Heinrich Schliemann (1822–1890), a wealthy German businessman and archeologist began excavating ancient Troy in 1868. When he found many swastika motifs there, he consulted Muller and another leading Sanskrit scholars. Muller identified the swastika for Schliemann as an "Aryan" symbol. In a lengthy reply to the archeologist discussing the symbol's meaning in ancient India, Muller wrote, "that among the Aryan nations the Swastika may have been an old emblem of the sun."[161] Muller's reference to "Aryan nations" appears to affirm a connection between Aryan and race, and through that connection a further identification with the swastika as a Proto-Indo-European symbol.

Another late 19th century swastika scholar, R.P. Greg, identified the swastika as "Aryan."[162] Greg expressed the opinion that the swastika is "far older and wider spread as a symbol than the triskelion [a three legged swastika], as well as being a more purely Aryan symbol."[163] His work was referred to in Wilson's definitive text on the swastika.

Emile Burnouf (1821–1907), of the French archaeological school in Athens, further assimilated the swastika into the Aryan myth. Burnouf claimed that it depicted the laying of sacred fires in Vedic India and was later adapted into the cross by Christianity. All of these scholars agreed that the swastika was an Aryan symbol.

Schliemann concluded that the swastika was a uniquely Indo-European or Aryan religious symbol connected with ancient migrations of Aryans. The swastika connected Aryans of the ancient West and the mysterious East. The swastika was henceforth launched as the Aryan symbol in the European mind.

"Aryan" did not at first clearly have a meaning of a superior race or racial discrimination in the late 19th century. "Aryan" primarily was seen then as the name of a Proto-Indo-European language and the people who spoke that language. The swastika was believed to be the Aryan symbol for the sun god, good luck, and auspiciousness. There is no reference from this period that associates the notion of "Aryan" and the "swastika" symbol with an idea of a master race or anti-Semitism.

However, the roots of that association began when Muller used the word "Aryan" as a term to describe the Proto-Indo-European language and speakers of this language. His arguments were crafted with a bias of European superiority that saw that which was not European as primitive and not advanced. By simply saying anything "good" must come from Europe or Germany, Aryan theory provided a convenient tool to steal goodness from Indian cultures. Though he contributed greatly to the fields of modern linguistics and Indian studies in Europe, Muller was also responsible for creating great misunderstandings and problems later for both India, through an incorrect representation of its history, and Europe because of his use of the word "Aryan." Muller, by strongly supporting the Aryan invasion myth of conquest by a superior light-skinned people of an inferior dark-skinned people in ancient India planted the seed of a superior Aryan race myth in Europe which paved the way later for Hitler's racist vision to be accepted. Muller knew the word "Aryan" was used frequently in Buddhist and Hindu texts. He translated many Buddhist texts including the *Dhammapada*. He was also aware of the frequent usage of the swastika in India as a symbol meaning sacred auspicious virtue. His misappropriation of the word "Aryan" set the course for the later damage done to this term as well as the swastika symbol, both sacred in Indian religions and culture, both now primarily understood in the current Western world as being associated with evil.

Both the Aryan notion and swastika symbol are very important for Buddhist, Hindu, and Jain religions and have been for thousands of years. To be an Aryan "noble" has been the goal of all Indian religions. Muller's work was careless and irresponsible toward the sacred religions and cultures of the East that he studied. It was also racist. By having Europeans take the credit for the Aryan language, all the great religions of India such as Buddhism, Hinduism, and Jain became a product of white "Aryan" people under his theories, which although they were only hypothetical, came to be accepted in the White Western world as historical reality.

[3] History of Aryan Superiority

In the 19th century, the term "Aryan" eventually came to be identified as a racial theory, rather than a language theory. European scholars such as Arthur de Gobineau, Ernst Ludwig Krause and Houston Stewart Chamberlain as well as the growing Occultist movement, each built upon Muller's work to further popularize and develop the idea of a superior "Aryan race."

Arthur de Gobineau (1816–1882), a mid-19th-century French diplomat, author, ethnologist, and racial theorist, in his writing *The Inequality of Human Races*, discussed Aryan superiority as a scientific theory and described Aryans as a superior race among white races. De Gobineau believed that civilization arose as the result of conquest by the superior Aryan race over inferior races. He listed ten civilizations, including Indian, Egyptian, Assyrian, and Chinese, and described all of them as either created or influenced by the Aryan race. De Gobineau divided races into three great races—white, yellow, and black.

Ernst Ludwig Krause (1839–1903), a popular German writer on

science, myth, and archaeology, was the first to link the Aryan swastika with German volkisch nationalism.[164] Racialism thus became identified with German nationalism. In the 19th century, it was a popular belief in Germany that each people have their own particular, superior genius that was expressed in their national spirit, which was called "Volksgeist."[165] German racialists, including the composer Richard Wagner, held that Nordic blood represented the best of the Aryan race.[166]

Houston Stewart Chamberlain (1855–1927), an Anglo-German author of philosophy and history, developed anti-Semitic racial theories based upon the concept of Aryan or Nordic superiority. His work *Foundation of the Nineteenth Century*, published in 1899, developed a theory of race and the dominant role of Germany that greatly influenced Hitler.[167] He wrote:

> Be that as it may, wherever the Aryans went they became masters. The Greek, the Latin, the Kelt, the Teuton, the Slav— all these were Aryans; of the aborigines of the countries which they overran, scarcely a trace remains. So, too, in India it was "Varna," colour, which distinguished the white conquering Arya from the defeated black man, the Dasyu, and so laid the foundation of caste. It is to the Teuton branch of the Aryan family that the first place in the world belongs, and the story of the Nineteenth Century is the story of the Teuton's triumph.[168]

The Aryan connection to the swastika was also popularized in Occultist movements including Theosophy, led by Helena P. Blavatsky (1831–1891), and later by Savitri Devi (1905–1982) and the Thule Society, which focused on the origins of the Aryan race.

By the time Hitler and his National Socialists were ready to ascend to power in the 1920s, the groundwork for Hitler's Nazi "Aryan" racial superiority theories had already long been laid in popular European perceptions of race, fueled by these scholars for whose work Muller's work served as a springboard.

The Meaning of "Aryan" for Hitler

How did Hitler understand the term "Aryan"? Judging from the usages of "Aryan" in *Mein Kampf*, Hitler interpreted the term to mean a Germanic white race, which he saw as a higher and superior race that created the great cultures and civilizations of the world. The intention in using the term Aryan was threefold—to affirm and praise Germanic blood and race with positive superior qualities; to affirm in comparison with lower races and Jews; and to win the fight against the Jews, whom Hitler described as the enemy of Aryans.

Gobineau's work influenced the development and popularity in Europe of the concept of Aryans as a superior race, though he himself was not anti-Semitic. The idea of Aryan supremacy was not always connected to anti-Semitism. Aryan superiority provided a feeling of confidence, affirmation, and pride to those who considered themselves Aryan. "Aryan" took on the meaning of a "chosen" race. Many Germans supported Hitler as the leader who would revitalize their fallen Germany, which lost World War I, and restore it to its imagined rightful place at the top of the world. Hitler inspired confidence and a sense of a superior identity in the German people through their shared "Aryan" identity, an identity expressed by and united under the lucky "Aryan" symbol, the Hakenkreuz-swastika.

In *Mein Kampf,* Hitler used the word "Aryan" often. It appears many times in Volume 1, Chapter 11, "Nation and Race," and throughout the work as well.

"Aryan" was used as an affirmation of the superior creativity of the German people:

> All the human culture, all the results of art, science, and technology that we see before us today, are almost exclusively the creative product of the **Aryan.** This very fact admits of the not unfounded inference that **he** alone was the founder of all higher humanity....[169]

> If we were to divide mankind into three groups, the founders of culture, the bearers of culture, the destroyers of culture, only the **Aryan** could be considered as the representative of the first group.[170]

> This mere sketch of the development of "culture-bearing: nations gives a picture of the growth, of the activity, and— the decline—of the true culture-founders of this earth, the **Aryans** themselves.[171]

Japanese culture too was a product of Aryan influence according to Hitler:

> The foundation of actual life is no longer the special Japanese culture, although it determined the color of life—because outwardly, in consequence of its inner differences, it is more conspicuous to the European—but gigantic scientific-techno-logical achievements of Europe and America; that is, **Aryan** people.[172]

> Therefore, just as the present Japanese development owes its life to **Aryan** origin, long ago in the gray past foreign influence and foreign spirit awakened the Japanese culture of that time.[173]

The Aryan of Hitler's imagination had a great personal quality of self-sacrifice for others, and ability to create great works for all human-kind, while at the same time not expecting much personal reward. Ary-ans work hard to bring benefit to all. This definition, which focuses on Aryan "noble" inner qualities, comes closest to the original Eastern understanding of Aryan. It is not clear though, whether or not that indi-cates awareness on Hitler's part of the Eastern definition of the term, or just an extension of his belief that Aryans were superior in every possible way. The difference of course is that for Hitler these noble inner qualities were naturally inborn and latent, but in the Eastern definition of "Aryan," nobility is only cultivated through practice of right thoughts and actions, and anyone has the potential to accomplish such practice.

> This self-sacrificing will to give one's personal labor and if necessary one's own life for others is most strongly devel-oped in the **Aryan**. The **Aryan** is not greatest in his mental qualities as such, but in the extent of his willingness to put all his abilities in the service of the community. In him the instinct of self-preservation has reached the noblest form... This state of mind, which subordinates the interests of the ego to the conservation of the community, is really the first premise for every truly human culture. From it alone can arise all the great works of mankind, which bring the founder little reward, but the richest blessings to posterity...[174]

> It is to this inner attitude that the **Aryan** owes his position in this world, and to it the world owes man; for it alone formed from pure spirit the creative force...[175]

The Aryan's relationship to other races is defined by Hitler as one of dominance as a leader or master of lower races. An Aryan needs to be assisted by others to complete the work of new cultural development. Aryans alone cannot accomplish building a culture. An Aryan is a conqueror of humanity:

> **Aryan** races—often absurdly small numerically—subject foreign peoples, and then stimulated by the special living conditions of the new territory (Fertility, Climatic conditions, etc.) and assisted by the multitude of lower-type beings standing at their disposal as helpers, develop the intellectual and organizational capacities dormant within them.[176]

> As soon as Fate leads [of the **Aryans**] toward special conditions, their latent abilities begin to develop in a more and more rapid sequence ... Without possibility of using the lower human beings, the **Aryan** would never have been able to take his first steps toward his future culture ... Hence it is no accident that the first cultures arose in places where the **Aryan**, in his encounters with lower peoples, subjugated them and bent them to his will. They then became the first technical instrument in the service of a developing culture. As long as he ruthlessly upheld the master attitude, not only did he really remain master, but also the preserver and increaser of culture.[177]

> Thus, the road which the **Aryan** had to take was clearly marked out. As a conqueror he subjected the lower beings and regulated their practical activity under his command, according to his will and for his aims.[178]

> Not in his intellectual gifts lies the source of the **Aryan**'s capacity for creating and building culture. If he had just this alone, he could only act destructively, in no case could he organize.[179]

Hitler considered purity of Aryan blood important. Mixing of Aryan blood with a lower race would lead to the destruction of cultures.

> No more than Nature desires the mating of weaker with stronger individuals, even less does she desire the blending of a higher with a lower race, since, if she did, her whole work of higher breeding, over perhaps hundreds of thousands of years, might be ruined with one blow. Historical experience offers countless proofs of this. It shows with terrifying clarity that in every mingling of **Aryan** blood with that of lower peoples the result was the end of the cultured people.[180]

> The **Aryan** gave up the purity of his blood and, therefore, lost
> his sojourn in the paradise within he had made for himself.
> He became submerged in the racial mixture, and gradually,
> more and more, lost his cultural capacity...[181]

The definition of the Aryan as a superior race necessitated an inferior opposing counterpart, as the existence of one extreme by definition necessitates its polar opposite. German people may have wondered if Aryans are superior, then why have Germans suffered? Hitler provided a convenient answer by faulting non-Aryans, especially Jews. This is where anti-Semitism appears in the development of Hitler's concept of Aryan. In some descriptions, Aryans are the victims of Jews. While Jews are described as intelligent, their abilities are not described as inborn like that of an Aryan, but rather something learned from "foreigners." Note the similarity between this idea and Aryan invasion theory, which posited that the superior culture found in India was not the result of native cultures but was rather introduced by a foreign other. Hitler continued to discuss Jews in relation to Aryans for the rest of the chapter over a span of thirty pages.

> The mightiest counterpart to the **Aryan** is represented by
> the Jew. In hardly any people in the world is the instinct
> of self-preservation developed more strongly than in the
> so-called "chosen." The mental qualities of the Jew have been
> schooled in the course of many centuries. Today he passes as
> "smart," and this in a certain sense he has been at all times.
> But his intelligence is not the result of his own development,
> but of visual instruction through foreigners.[182]

For Hitler, the Aryan represents God, the creator, and goodness; the Jew represents Demons, the destroyer or evil, both in an eternal fight. Hitler's struggle is a struggle between himself and Aryans vs. Jews.

> And assuredly this world is moving toward a great revolution.
> The question can only be whether it will redound to the bene-
> fit of **Aryan** humanity or to the profit of the eternal Jew.[183]

> The organizing principle of **Aryan** humanity is replaced by
> the destructive principle of the Jew. He becomes a ferment of
> decomposition among peoples and races, and in the broader
> sense a dissolver of human culture.[184]

In any case the Jew reached his desired goal: Catholics and
Protestants wage a merry war with one another, and the mor-
tal enemy of **Aryan** humanity and all Christendom laughs up
his sleeve.[185]

In Hitler's time, it was believed among racial theorists that within
the larger Aryan race, there were different sub-Aryan races. Of these, the
Aryan-Nordic, from which Germans were said to be directly descended,
were seen by Hitler and others as the original, purest Aryans, the highest
among all other Aryan races. Encouraged by Heinrich Himmler, Hitler
endorsed research about Aryans and sent an expedition team to Lhasa
in Tibet in 1938–1939. One of the goals of the expedition was to prove
that Aryans were the mother race of the Tibetans, which would make it
possible to claim Nordic racial hegemony for the entire Indo-European
world. The expedition collected cranial measurements of native Tibetans
and samples of local plant and animal species. Tibetan cultural traditions
were also observed. The expedition was cut short by the outbreak of war
in Europe and the team returned to Germany, where they were warmly
greeted by Himmler.[186]

For Hitler, the term Aryan represented that which is good, noble, and
heroic. His definition appropriated the meaning of noble and venerable
whether knowingly or unknowingly, in its reference to positive inner
qualities. However, describing Aryan as a master race meant to lord over
others, with Jews as a polar opposite enemy, was certainly ignoble, and in
creating this definition, Hitler created a meaning antithetical to the original one. There is no such thing as Aryan blood. In the Eastern understanding, anybody can become an Aryan when he/she lives a wholesome
"noble" life.

The Aryan race wasn't generally seen as an Asian race by Hitler with
the exception of Japanese, but as a white race that conquered and was
meant to dominate Asia and other parts of the world. Likewise, Hitler
saw the swastika, not as a native Asian symbol, but as a Western one
brought to Asia by Western conquerors.

When Hitler used the Hook-Cross as the emblem for the Aryan-man,
he saw it as a symbol of a Christian Aryan race. When describing the
early National Socialist flag design, Hitler wrote that one could see elements of the party's program in it, including, "In the *swastika* [Haken-
kreuz] the mission of the struggle for the victory of the **Aryan** man."[187]

The association of Hitler's Aryans with the Christian cross might have emerged from Houston Chamberlain's influence. In *Foundation of the Nineteenth Century*, Houston wrote:

> For—however unworthy we may show ourselves of this—our whole culture, thank God, still stands under the sign of the Cross upon Golgotha. We do see this Cross; but who sees the Crucified One? Yet He, and He alone is the living well of all Christianity, ... Christ was still greater. And like the everlasting "hearth-fire" of the Aryans, so the torch of the truth which He kindled for us can never be extinguished.[188]

Chamberlain argued that Jesus was not really a Jew, but descendent from the Aryan race. He explained Jesus's "purely Aryan blood"[189] was carried by ancestors who migrated to Galilee from the Phoenicians and Greeks whom he claimed were "Aryan Armenians":

> Whoever makes the assertion that Christ was a Jew is either ignorant or insincere: ignorant when he confuses religion and race, insincere when he knows the history of Galilee and partly conceals, partly distorts the very entangled facts in favour of his religious prejudices or, it may be, to curry favour with the Jews. The probability that Christ was no Jew, that He had not a drop of genuinely Jewish blood in his veins, is so great that it is almost equivalent to a certainty.[190]

Seen in this way, Hitler's swastika-cross emblem takes on the added meaning of victory for "an Aryan-Christian" race, an affirmation for Germans as a proud Aryan-Christian people.

Hitler used the new symbol as propaganda to create a positive image of this superior Aryan race. Post cards and stamps from Nazi Germany portrayed the Hook-Cross as the sun, bringing hope and light to the German people (Figs. 98–100).[191]

Though it has been a matter of historical debate whether or not Hitler himself truly believed in Christianity, it is clear that he saw German churches as a propaganda vehicle to promote the Third Reich. In May 1933, Ludwig Muller was appointed by Hitler and became a single Reich Bishop (*Reichsbischof*) as part of the Nazi plan to coordinate all twenty-eight Protestant churches into a single Reich Church, supported by German Christians (*Deutsche Christen*). At the National Reich Church,

98. Nazi postcard showing a Hook-Cross as the sun.

99. Poster stamp. 6th Country Rally, 1939, Danish Nazi Party.

100. Nazi airmail stamp (1934).

the crucifix was replaced by the Hakenkreuz-swastika symbol, and the Bible was replaced by a copy of *Mein Kampf*, kept on the altar alongside a sword. Already established Protestant Churches were later encouraged to do the same as part of a thirty-point plan to take over Protestant churches, and some did, though not all churches went along with the plan.[192]

In July 1933, a concordat was signed and sealed by Eugenio Pacelli (later Pope Pius XII) and Franz von Papen (Hitler's Vice-Chancellor), which defined Hitler's relationship to the Catholic Church. Keeping good relations with the nearly 40 million Protestants and 20 million Catholics in Germany, which combined represented approximately 90% of the population, was essential for the success of the Third Reich. The majority of both Catholics and Protestants became supporters of Nazi Germany.[193] Approximately 525,000 Jews lived in Germany, which was less than 1% of Germany's total population of 66 million at the time.[194]

The following is a passage from a Christmas sermon delivered in a Lutheran and Reformed Church in Solgen, Germany, in 1936. Through it we can see how central the Hakenkreuz was to Hitler's vision and the propaganda through which that vision was expressed:

Germany, after the Great War, was threatened with collapse. But then he came who, despite the great darkness in so many German hearts, spoke of light and showed them the way to the light. His appeal found an echo in thousands and hundreds of thousands of German souls, who carried the appeal further. It swelled out like a sweeping cloud and then happened that greatest miracle: Germany awoke and followed the sign of light, the Hakenkreuz [Hook-Cross].

The darkness is now conquered, now suffering is over, which so long gripped our people. The Sun is rising ever higher, with our ancient German symbol, the Hakenkreuz, and its warmth surrounds the whole German people, melts our hearts together into one great German community. No one is left out, no one needs to hunger or freeze, despite the deep night and snow and ice because the warmth from the hearts of the whole people pours out, in the emblems of the National Socialist Welfare programme and the Winter Help work and carries the German Xmas in the most forsaken German heart.

In this hour, Adolf Hitler is our benefactor, who has overcome the winter night with its terrors for the whole people and has led us under the Hakenkreuz to a new light and a new day."[195]

This quote shows how Hitler appropriated the Hakenkreuz's image in the East as a symbol of good fortune and the sun. In this quote, the symbol takes on a mystical quality. It has moved beyond simply expressing the political ideology of the National Socialists and now encapsulates all of Germany's hopes, destiny, and birthright as the Aryan nation, chosen by God to lead the world, under a heavenly mandate. It has merged with Nazi Germany's expression of German Christianity. Although it has appropriated the good luck meaning from its Eastern origins, it is no longer an Asian symbol. The Hakenkreuz is understood as a new/ancient symbol of Germany.

But it had also moved beyond being just a Christian cross, becoming the symbol of the new state religion of Nazism. It became a new kind of cross under which this new nation of Aryans that Hitler imagined and was constructing could be united.

FIVE

Hitler's Second Meaning of "Hakenkreuz": Anti-Semitism

As National Socialists, we see our program in our flag ... in the Haken-kreuz [Hook-Cross], ... by the same token, ... the mission of the struggle for ... the victory of the idea of creative work, which as such always has been and always will be anti-Semitic.

Mein Kampf

Meaning of Anti-Semitism

The second assigned meaning of the Hakenkreuz symbol is the victory of anti-Semitism, as Hitler clearly stated in *Mein Kampf*. It is very difficult to associate the Eastern swastika symbol with anti-Semitism anywhere in its historical usage beyond the Nazi era. However once Hitler's symbol is understood as a "Hook-Cross," a kind of Christian cross, then the association with anti-Semitism is clearer, as anti-Semitism has been an ongoing part of Christian history.

"Anti-Semitism" is defined by the *Oxford English Dictionary* (1989) as "theory, action, or practice directed against the Jews," and "anti-Sem-ite" as "one who is hostile or opposed to the Jews." Some scholars prefer to make a distinction between discrimination against religious belief (anti-Judaism) and racial discrimination (anti-Semitism) when discussing anti-Jewish prejudice. I chose to use the general term "anti-Semitism," which can include both religious and racial prejudice. When I need to make distinctions, I simply use such phrases as religious anti-Semitism, racial anti-Semitism, economic anti-Semitism, etc. Moreover, Hitler used the word *Antisemite (n), Antisemitisch, Antisemitismus* (anti-Semite, anti-Semitic, or anti-Semitism) but not "anti-Judaism." The German word *Antisemitisch* was first used in 1860 in relation to the "Aryan" race.[196]

Hitler explains clearly in *Mein Kampf* that his Hook-Cross was meant to be a symbol of both the victory of Aryan man, as well as the victory of anti-Semitism. The Third Reich would be a Germany in which Jews, the true cause of Aryan German suffering and defeat in his vision, were exterminated. Hitler's *Mein Kampf* says,

> As National Socialists, we see our program in our flag... in the Hook-Cross the mission of the struggle for the victory of the Aryan man, and, by the same token, the victory of the idea of creative work, which as such always has been and always will be anti-Semitic.[197]

Hitler's incorporation of the Hook-Cross in his anti-Semitic plan was another step on a long road of the Christian cross's use for militant anti-Semitism in other previous periods of Western history. Hitler was not the first to introduce anti-Semitism to Germany, where it had a lengthy history in association with Christianity.[198] Though the term "anti-Semitism" was introduced in the 19th century, discrimination and hostility against Jews and Judaism had existed in European history in relation to Christianity since at least the late 1st century, when the New Testament was written. The New Testament helped propagate negative images of Jews, especially the Gospel of John, which describes Jews as associated with darkness and the devil, and as Jesus's opponents.[199] After the 2nd century, many churches began to preach about Jews as a rejected and despised people, fated to live a deservedly marginal and miserable life, because Jews rejected and killed the Messiah. In some European countries, Jews were marginalized in society, and sometimes also physically attacked.

Theodosius I, the Roman emperor (379–395), decreed Christianity (Orthodox Nicene Christianity) to be the official state religion of the Roman Empire in A.D. 380. Christianity then became the dominant religion in Europe. Inspired by the 4th-century Roman Empire, the Carolingian renaissance in the late 8th century further developed Christian culture through literature, art, music, and architecture. The flourishing of Christianity in society often meant more difficulties for Jews, as the further spread of Christianity's negative characterization of Jews invited greater hostility toward Jews.

In the Middle Ages, during the first crusade, a military campaign to recover the Holy Land from the Muslims in 1095, led by the Latin Roman Catholic Church under Pope Urban II, turned bloodshed into a sacred act. Though Muslims were the main target, Jews were also seen as enemies of Christ and were violently attacked by Christian mobs on their way to Jerusalem. Known as the Rhineland Massacres, hundreds of thousands of Jews were killed. Historian Albert of Aix in the 11th century described the massacres:

> Emicho and the rest of his troop consulted together, and at daybreak they attacked the Jews in the palace with arrows and spears, broke bolts and doors, and overcame and killed about seven hundred of the Jews as they tried in vain to withstand the strength and attack of so many thousands. They slaughtered the women in just the same say, and cut down with their swords found children, whatever their age and sex. The Jew, indeed, seeing how the Christian enemy were rising up against them and their little children and were sparing none of any age, even turned upon themselves and their companions, on children, women, mothers and sisters, and they all killed each other. Mothers with children at the breast—how horrible to relate—would cut their throats with knives, would stab others, preferring that they should die thus at their hands, rather than be killed by the weapons of the uncircumcised.[200]

Violence against Jews has a long history in Europe. These massacres were rooted in the idea of fighting against an enemy of Christ, an enemy of his or her own God or belief. The theological anti-Judaism of the Church during the medieval and Reformation periods provided a strong historical foundation for an anti-Semitism that solidified over time in modern Europe. The Jews of Germany in particular were subjected to many prejudices and brutality. Martin Luther's written work, *On the Jews and their Lies*,[201] later furthered the anti-Jewish sentiment in Germany. Hitler's anti-Semitism did not appear all of a sudden in a vacuum, but rather resulted from waves of anti-Semitism throughout European history, deeply rooted in Christianity.

In Hitler's choice of the Hook-Cross or Hakenkreuz for his flag, we can see Hitler's attempt to portray himself to the nation as a dedicated Christian leader against evil forces. In *Mein Kampf* Hitler proclaimed: "Hence today I believe that I am acting in accordance with the will of the Almighty Creator: by defending myself against the Jew, I am fighting for the work of the Lord."[202] This statement suggests Hitler's intent to raise the flag of his new Cross, the Hook-Cross, under which he would be a sacred fighter for Jesus Christ, following the will of God and with His divine mandate.

Anti-Semitism and Hitler's Early Life

Hitler's personal journey into anti-Semitism began when he arrived from Linz in Vienna, Austria, in 1907 to apply for art school and, as he described in *Mein Kampf,* "encountered the Jewish questions." He recalled, " There were few Jews in Linz. In the course of the centuries their outward appearance had become Europeanized and had taken on a human look; in fact, I even took them for Germans."[203]

When Hitler saw Jews with "a black caftan and black hair locks" in Vienna for the first time, he asked himself, "Is this a Jew?" and then, "Is this a German?[204] These questions led him to explore anti-Semitic viewpoints. Hitler said he occasionally picked up the *Deutsches Volksblatta,* a German American newspaper, when he was in Vienna. "I was not in agreement with the sharp anti-Semitic tone, but from time to time I read arguments which gave me some food for thought," he wrote.[205] Through these readings he became acquainted with Dr. Karl Lueger, leader of the Christian Social Party movement.

When Hitler initially arrived in Vienna, he was in opposition to Dr. Lueger and the Party, both of which he felt were reactionary. But as Hitler became more familiar with Dr. Lueger and the movement, he grew to admire them. Hitler wrote,

> Today, more than ever, I regard this man [Dr. Lueger] as the greatest German mayor of all times. How many of my basic principles were upset by this change in my attitude toward the Christian Social movement! My views with regard to anti-Semitism thus succumbed to the passage of time, and this was my great transformation of all.[206]

According to *Mein Kampf,* Hitler evaluated two anti-Semitic movements in Vienna at that time: The Christian Socialists under Karl Lueger, and the Pan-Germans under Georg von Schonerer. Hitler described his feelings about Schonerer:

> Nevertheless my personal sympathy lay at first on the side of the Pan-German Schonerer ... Compared as to abilities, Schonerer seemed to me even then the better and more profound thinker in questions of principle. He foresaw the inevitable end of the Austrian state more clearly and correctly than anyone else.... But if Schonerer recognized the problems in their innermost essence, he erred when it came to men.[207]

Hitler was drawn to Schonerer's ideology and Dr. Lueger's Christian Socialist political attitude, which he would later combine to form the anti-Semitic ideology of Nazi Germany.

Hitler's anti-Semitism did not arise suddenly and spontaneously from within himself, but was instead a gradual process of absorbing ideas through his surroundings, including the Christian Socialist movement. Individuals and the larger Christian society influenced Hitler in the formation and development of his ideas of a master race and anti-Semitism.

Hitler was a great admirer of Martin Luther, Richard Wagner, as well as Frederick the Great. The first two, Luther and Wagner, were both anti-Jewish, though Frederick was not. In *Mein Kampf* he praised them in a chapter titled "The Beginning of My Political Activities," describing them as "great warriors in this world, who, though not understood by the present, are nevertheless prepared to carry the fight for their ideas and ideals to the end...To them belong, not only the truly great statesmen, but all other great reformers as well. Beside Frederick the Great stands Martin Luther as well as Richard Wagner."[208] Hitler praised them as "three of our greatest Germans" *(Wir kennen drei deutsche Männer, die wahrhaft groß gewesen sind)* in his speech at Nuremberg in October 1923.[209]

Hitler's own anti-Semitism is inextricably intertwined with the anti-Semitism of those who influenced him, who in turn were influenced by a longer history of Christian, and specifically German Christian anti-Semitism. It is important to understand this to perceive why Hitler constructed his version of the swastika as a cross in continuity with these influences.

Martin Luther (1483–1546)

In 1933, the Hook-Cross was officially adopted as the new German Christian cross at a conference held at Castle Church in Wittenberg, the cathedral where Martin Luther had begun the Protestant Reformation movement four hundred years earlier. The Hook-Cross was now considered a symbol of German Christianity, which meant that all Christians in Germany were required to use the Hook-Cross, replacing the standard Christian cross or crucifix. Many churches displayed the Hook-Cross on their altars. The German church was not neutral but largely supported the anti-Jewish movement openly or quietly. German church leaders enthusiastically dived into the growing anti-Semitic tide, claiming the mandate to do so from Luther's teachings.[210] A German pastor wrote to a German newspaper in 1935:

> We stand enthusiastically behind your struggle against the Jewish death watch beetles which are undermining our German nation... So too against those friends of Jewry which are found even in the ranks of the Protestant pastorate. We will fight along side of you and we will not give up until the struggle against all Jewry and against the murderers of Our Savior has been brought to a victorious end, in the Spirit of Christ and of Martin Luther. In true fellowship, I greet you with Heil Hitler![211]

Bishop Martin Sasse, a leading German Protestant, published a compilation of Martin Luther's anti-Semitic writings shortly after *Kristallnacht*. In the Foreword, Sasse praised the burning of the synagogues and the coincidence of the day the violence occurred. "On November 10, 1938, on Luther's birthday, the synagogues are burning in Germany." He encouraged German people to keep in mind the words "of the greatest anti-Semite of his time, the warner of his people against the Jews."[212] Martin Luther was clearly seen as anti-Semitic even in Hitler's time. Luther's work *"Von den Juden und ihren Lügen"* (On the Jews and Their Lies) (1543) contains very strong views against Jews spanning more than 100 pages.

Martin Luther was a prominent theologian and Augustinian monk best know for writing the "95 Theses" in 1517, which would later form the basis for the Protestant Reformation. He was a Biblical scholar who translated the Old Testament from Hebrew and the New Testament from

Greek into German, which contributed to the development of the German language. He was one of the most influential Christian leaders in German history. When he was in his 40s, Luther stood against anti-Semitism in society and Catholicism. Later he changed his views and became disappointed that Jews were not converting to Christianity. He became a strong anti-Semite and wrote *On the Jews and Their Lies*, at the age of 60. Luther's harsh rhetoric had a significant impact on Germany and the development of Hitler's hatred toward Jews.

Luther explained that his beliefs about Jews were based upon the Old and New Testament. However, Luther described Jews as a "brood of vipers," children of Satan rather than Abraham's children. He said:

> No one can take away from them their pride concerning their blood and their descent from Israel. In the Old Testament they lost many a battle in wars over this matter, though no Jew understands this. All the prophets censured them for it, for it betrays an arrogant, carnal presumption devoid of spirit and of faith. They were also slain and persecuted for this reason. St. John the Baptist took them to task severely because of it, saying, "Do not presume to say to yourselves, 'We have Abraham for our father'; for I tell you, God is able from these stones to raise up children to Abraham" [Matt. 3:9]. He did not call them Abraham's children but a "brood of vipers" [Matt. 3:7]. Oh, that was too insulting for the noble blood and race of Israel, and they declared, "He has a demon" [Matt. 11:18]. Our Lord also calls them a "brood of vipers"; furthermore, in John 3:39[213] he states: "If you were Abraham's children, you would do what Abraham did.... You are of your father the devil." It was intolerable to them to hear that they were not Abraham's but the devil's children, nor can they bear to hear this today. If they should surrender this boast and argument, their whole system which is built on it would topple and change.[214]

Hitler used the term "viper" to refer to Jews, writing, "The man who has never been in the clutches of that crushing viper can never know what its poison is."[215] "Occasionally, when bitten, they imprisoned one or another journalistic viper for a few weeks or months, but the whole poisonous brood was allowed to carry on in peace."[216] Luther warned Christians not to allow themselves to be confused by Jews.

Learn from this dear Christian, what you are doing if you per-
mit the blind Jews to mislead you. Then the saying will truly
apply, 'When a blind man leads a blind man, both will fall into
the pit" [cf. Luke 6:39]. You cannot learn anything from them
except how to misunderstand the divine commandments,
and, despite this, boast haughtily over against the Gentiles
who really are much better before God than they, since they
do not have such pride of holiness and yet keep far more of
the law than these arrogant saints and damned blasphemers
and liars.[217]

Luther blamed the Jews for the crucifixion of the Messiah Jesus. He
preached that Jews are guilty of the death of Christ, and John's gospel
considered the Jews as enemies of Jesus. As Luther writes:

Now as I began to ask earlier: What harm has the poor Jesus
done to the most holy children of Israel that they cannot stop
cursing him after his death, with which he paid his debt? Is it
perhaps that he aspires to be the Messiah, which they cannot
tolerate? Oh no, for he is dead. They themselves crucified
him, and a dead person cannot be the Messiah. Perhaps he is
an obstacle to their return into their homeland? No, that is
not the reason either; for how can a dead man prevent that?
What, then, is the reason? I will tell you. As I said before, it is
the lightning and thunder of Moses to which I referred before:
"The Lord will smite you with madness and blindness and
confusion of mind." It is the eternal fire of which the prophets
speak: "My wrath will go forth like fire, and burn with none
to quench it" [Jer. 4:4]. John the Baptist proclaimed the same
message to them after Herod had removed their scepter, saying [Luke 3:17]: "His winnowing fork is in his hand, and he will
clear his threshing-floor and gather his wheat into his granary,
but his chaff he will burn with unquenchable fire." Indeed,
such fire of divine wrath we behold descending on the Jews.
We see it burning, ablaze and aflame, a fire more horrible
than that of Sodom and Gomorrah.[218]

Hitler saw the presence of Jews in society to have catastrophic conse-
quences. This is similar to Luther's view. Hitler said,

They (many people) close their eyes in reverend abhorrence
to this godless scourge and pray to the Almighty that He—if

possible after their own death—may rain down fire and brimstone as on Sodom and Gomorrah and so once again make an outstanding example of this shameless section of humanity.[219]

If Hitler's fight is at least in part a Christian crusade against Jews, it is logical for his flag to reflect the Christian Cross, built upon the foundation of Luther's religious anti-Semitism.

Luther gave concrete advice to fellow Christians about what should be done with the Jews. Luther gave seven pieces of advice, the first of which chillingly foretold and perhaps inspired *Kristallnacht,* the pogrom that occurred in Germany and Austria between November 8 and 10, 1938, during which the Nazis murdered Jews, shattered glass store windows, and destroyed hundreds of synagogues and Jewish-owned businesses, leaving the streets covered with broken glass—just as Luther proposed centuries earlier.

First, to set fire to their synagogues or schools and to bury and cover with dirt whatever will not burn, so that no man will ever again see a stone or cinder of them. This is to be done in honor of our Lord and of Christendom, so that God might see that we are Christians, and do not condone or knowingly tolerate such public lying, cursing, and blaspheming of his Son and of his Christians....[220]

Second, I advise that their houses also be razed and destroyed. For they pursue in them the same aims as in their synagogues.....

Third, I advise that all their prayer books and Talmudic writings, in which such idolatry, lies, cursing, and blasphemy are taught, be taken from them....

Fourth, I advise that their rabbis be forbidden to teach henceforth on pain of loss of life and limb....

Fifth, I advise that safe-conduct on the highways be abolished completely for the Jews....

Sixth, I advise that usury be prohibited to them, and that all cash and treasure of silver and gold be taken from them and put aside for safekeeping....

Seventh, I recommend putting a flail, an ax, a hoe, a spade, a distaff, or a spindle into the hands of young, strong Jews and

> Jewesses and letting them earn their bread in the sweat of
> their brow, as was imposed on the children of Adam....[221]

Luther offered advice to Christian pastors and preachers as well as government authorities to "be on their guard against Jews." The Institute for the Study and Eradication of Jewish Influence on German Church Life celebrated its official opening at Wartburg Castle on May 6, 1939. The Institute, supported by many Christian theologians, pastors, and church-goers, aimed to develop Christian theology free from Jewish-influenced Christianity. In other words, the Institute was a realization of Luther's suggestions to pastors about four hundred years earlier. In Nazi Germany, citizens were "called upon to be the victors in Jesus's own struggle against the Jews, who were said to be seeking Germany's destruction."[222] Many churches in Germany placed the Hakenkreuz symbol at their altars without much hesitation, because it was another Christian cross symbol, not something different and exotic imported from another religion. The state and religion were seen as an organic whole, as Luther appealed to both religious leaders and government authority against Jews. Hitler achieved this by filling Germany with the Hakenkreuz cross emblem.

> And you, my dear gentlemen and friends who are pastors
> and preachers, I wish to remind very faithfully of your official
> duty, so that you too may warn your parishioners concerning
> their eternal harm, as you know how to do, namely, that they
> be on their guard against the Jews and avoid them so far as
> possible ... much more leave our Lord the Messiah, our faith,
> and our church undefiled and uncontaminated with their dev-
> ilish tyranny and malice.... let us follow the advice of Christ
> (Matthew 10:14) and shake the dust from our shoes, and say,
> "We are innocent of your blood."[223]

There are many more anti-Semitic passages in Luther's text, but the last quotation from the very last paragraph of *On The Jews and Their Lies* provides a powerful and chilling endnote in that it sets the stage for, justifies, and encourages conflict between Jews and Christians through its identification of Christians as the rightful "foe" of devilish Jews.

> So long an essay, dear sir and good friend, you have elicited
> from me with your booklet in which a Jew demonstrates his

skill in a debate with an absent Christian. He would not, thank God, do this in my presence! My essay, I hope, will furnish a Christian (who in any case has no desire to become a Jew) with enough material not only to defend himself against the blind, venomous Jews, but also to become the foe of the Jews' malice, lying, and cursing, and to understand not only that their belief is false but that they are surely possessed by all devils. May Christ, our dear Lord, convert them mercifully and preserve us steadfastly and immovably in the knowledge of him, which is eternal life. Amen.[224]

Martin Luther's views toward Jews became part of the foundation of Hitler's anti-Semitism.

Since the Jew is not the attacked but the attacker, not only anyone who attacks passes as his enemy, but also anyone who resists him. But the means with which he seeks to break such reckless but upright souls is not honest warfare, but lies and slander. Here he stops at nothing, and in his vileness he becomes so gigantic that no one need be surprised if among our people the personification of the devil as the symbol of all evil assumes the living shape of the Jew. The ignorance of the broad masses about the inner nature of the Jew, the lack of instinct and narrow-mindedness of our upper classes, make the people an easy victim for this Jewish campaign of lies.[225]

Luther, writing in *An Open Letter on the Harsh Book,* justifies the action of killing for the purpose of stopping evil and maintaining "peace and safety." Luther writes:

Therefore, as I wrote then so I write now; Let no one have mercy on the obstinate, hardened, blinded peasants who refuse to listen to reason; but let everyone, as he is able, strike, hew, stab, and slay, as though among mad dogs, put to flight, and led astray by these peasants, so that peace and safety may be maintained.

The merciless punishment of the wicked is not being carried out just to punish the wicked and make them atone for the evil desires that are in their blood, but to protect the righteous and to maintain peace and safety. And beyond all doubt, these are precious works of mercy, love, and kindness…[226]

From this point of view, the Holocaust could be justified by Hitler as a sacred mission against evil, an as an act of love and kindness with a noble purpose, rather that an evil act. History teaches us that human beings are capable of killing and committing great evil in the name of their own distorted views of justice and righteousness. Sometimes we hear, "how could any human being do such evil as was done by Hitler?" Yet all human beings are capable of doing such when certain conditions are fulfilled. Neither Luther nor Hitler saw their actions as evil, but rather as acts of heroic righteousness to stop evil, based upon their interpretation of Christianity. Hitler's speeches show how Luther's anti-Semitic interpretation of Christianity influenced Hitler, and how Hitler interpreted Christianity in the context of his socio-political movement. In a speech given in Munich in April 1922, Hitler said:

> My feeling as a Christian points me to my Lord and Savior as a fighter. It points me to the man who once in loneliness, surrounded by a few followers, recognized these Jews for what they were and summoned men to fight against them and who, God's truth! was greatest not as a sufferer but as a fighter. In boundless love as a Christian and as a man I read through the passage which tells us how the Lord at last rose in His might and seized the scourge to drive out of the Temple the brood of vipers and adders. How terrific was His fight for the world against the Jewish poison. To-day, after two thousand years, with deepest emotion I recognize more profoundly than ever before the fact that it was for this that He had to shed His blood upon the Cross. As a Christian I have no duty to allow myself to be cheated, but I have the duty to be a fighter for truth and justice... And if there is anything which could demonstrate that we are acting rightly it is the distress that daily grows. For as a Christian I have also a duty to my own people.[227]

It is also important to realize these actions Luther suggested were based upon the idea of defending Christianity. The Nazis' violence toward Jews was done with the goal of a Christian victory in what Hitler possibly saw as an inevitable conflict between Christians and Jews, a Nazi victory represented by the Nazi symbol of the Nazi Hook-Cross.

As Hitler's movement was influenced by Luther's views, it should be no surprise that the symbol of that movement would have likewise evolved from Christianity's central symbol, the cross. Yet, although many scholars have explored the Lutheran Christian influence on Hitler, they have failed to note the cross within the swastika shape. By recognizing the cross within Hitler's swastika, we can see Hitler's Nazi movement as a continuation of an earlier anti-Jewish movement in German Christianity.

Richard Wagner (1813–1883)

Hitler once said, "Whoever wants to understand National Socialist Germany must know Wagner."[228] From the time of his youth, Hitler worshiped and idolized Wagner. Even after becoming Chancellor of Germany, Hitler continued to be a great fan of Wagner. Every year, Hitler attended the Bayreuth Festival[229] of Wagnerian opera and declared it a National Socialist annual event. Hitler never tired of Wagner's operas. In a speech given on November 3, 1923, Hitler said, "The reason we perceive the artist Richard Wagner as being great is because he represented heroic folklore, Germanness, in all his works. The Heroic is the Great. That is what our people long for."[230]

Hitler also visited Wagner's home many times. By the time Hitler was born in 1889, Wagner was already dead. Hitler never met Wagner physically, but connected through his music and writings.

Richard Wagner may have been the key inspiration for Hitler's new Hakenkreuz emblem. Hitler's concepts of the "victory of Aryan man," as well as the anti-Semitic "victory of the idea of creative work," arose from the influence of Wagner's words and creations. Both of these concepts are the central meanings of Hitler's Hook-Cross symbol.

[1] Hitler's Encounter with Wagner

In *Mein Kampf* Hitler writes of his first experience with Wagnerian opera, a viewing of *Lohengrin*.

> I was captivated at once. My youthful enthusiasm for the master of Bayreuth knew no bounds. Again and again I was drawn to his works, and it still seems to me especially fortunate that the modest provincial performance left me open to an intensified experience later on.[231]

Siegfried, the fearless Germanic hero of Wagner's opera *Nibelungen,* is referred to in Hitler's *Mein Kampf.* Hitler's reference to Siegfried is meant as a personification of Germany itself. Hitler wrote:

> The International Jewish world finance needed these lures to enable it to carry out its long-desired plan for destroying Germany which thus far did not submit to its widespread superstate control of finance and economics. Only in this way could they forge a coalition made strong and courageous by the sheer numbers of the gigantic armies now on the march and prepared to attack the horny Siegfried at last.[232]

August Kubizek met Adolf Hitler in either 1904 or 1905 at the opera. Because of their mutual interest in the opera, a friendship developed. They went to the opera together many times over four years. Kubizek explained Hitler's enthusiasm for Wagner in the book *The Young Hitler I Knew.*

> Listening to Wagner meant to him [Hitler], not a simple visit to the theatre but the opportunity of being transported into that extraordinary state which Wagner's music produced in him, that trance, that escape into the mystical dream world which he needed in order to sustain the enormous tension of his turbulent nature.... Of course, we knew by heart *Lohengrin,* Adolf's favorite opera—I believe he saw it ten times during our time together in Vienna—and the same is true of *Meistersinger....* For him nothing counted but German ways, German feeling and German thought. He accepted none but the German masters. How often did he tell me that he was proud to belong to a people who had produced such masters.... His devotion to, and veneration of Wagner took almost the form of a religion. When he listened to Wagner's music he was a changed man: his violence left him, he became quiet, yielding and tractable. His gaze lost its restlessness; his own destiny, however heavily it may have weighed upon him, became unimportant. He no longer felt lonely and outlawed, misjudged by society. As if intoxicated by some hypnotic agent, he slipped into a state of ecstasy, and willingly let himself be carried away into that mystical universe which was more real to him than the actual workaday world. From the stale, musty prison of his back room, he was transported into the blissful regions of Germanic antiquity, that ideal world which was the lofty goal for all his endeavours.[233]

Judging from Kubizek's recollections, Wagner for Hitler was not just an impetus for political ideology, but also his private place of refuge, the source of his energy and spiritual comfort. Kubizek noted how Hitler changed while listening to Wagner, becoming more focused and calm, and almost hypnotized. They also went to other operas, but Hitler did not care much for them.

Hitler decided to become a politician after he saw Wagner's *Rienzi* for his first time. Encountering Rienzi made young Hitler recognize the path of politics distinct from artist, painter, and architect Hitler. Kubizek shared that unforgettable day of Hitler's decision at the heights of the Freinberg Mountain in Linz.

> It was a state of complete ecstasy and rapture, in which he transferred the character of Rienzi, without even mentioning him as a model or example with visionary power, to the plan of his own ambitions. But it was more than a cheap adaptation; the impact of the opera was rather a sheer external impulse which compelled him to speak. Like flood waters breaking their dykes, his words burst forth from him. He conjured up in grandiose, inspiring pictures his own future and that of his people.[234]

Wagner was considered one of the great German composers, and was especially known for his operas. His style of opera was often described as a musical drama. Wagner strove to create a "total work of art" fusing music, poetry, and spectacular visual effects with a dramatic storyline. Wagner considered his music to be essentially German, with lyrics written in German. His operas were filled with German-centered elements such as Teutonic, Nordic, and German mythology, and heroic tales. This sense of German-ness was Wagner's essence. He believed German people had an innate German spirit, which he always celebrated and praised in his work. His masterpiece *Der Ring des Nibelungen* moved German audiences with a sense of a German-centered universe. Other works included *Lohengrin, Dei Meistersinger, Die fliegende Hollander, Tannhauser, Tristan und Isolde,* and *Parsifal.*

Hitler's theatrical presentations at political events were influenced by Wagner's concept of a "Total Work of Art." As the propaganda film *Triumph of the Will* (1935) by Leni Riefenstahl shows, Hitler brought excitement to political events. For Hitler, politics were operatic theater. A Hitler rally featured more than a good speech. It was also a thrilling spectacle of Wagnerian theatrics including music, fireworks, parades, torchlight processions, and music, usually by Wagner. And of course Hook-Cross flags, which served as an essential element in the set, providing a powerful, dominating visual symbol for all to adopt and unite behind.

Wagner was influential for Hitler not only through his music but also through his philosophy and political ideas that included anti-Semitic views. Wagner suffered in many ways throughout his life despite his great achievements. He lived a free, untraditional lifestyle, and expressed controversial views toward German society, religion, and politics. He was often plagued by financial difficulties and lived part of his life in exile. A libretto of *Der Ring des Nibelungen* and the anti-Semitic article *Judaism in Music* were written when Wagner was forced to live in exile in Switzerland on the run from his participation in the 1849 Dresden revolution. Wagner's difficult and tumultuous life was somewhat similar to Hitler's life. Hitler wrote his own major work, *Mein Kampf,* while he was in prison at Landsberg Castle in Munich following his own failed attempt at German revolution. Wagner in both his life story and his music was a person with whom Hitler could identify, and therefore be influenced by.

[2] *"Judaism in Music"* and Anti-Semitism

Wagner was an unabashed anti-Semite. He once said, "I felt a long-repressed hatred for this Jewry, and this hatred is as necessary to my nature as gall is to the blood."[235] Oddly, although he often expressed aggressive anti-Jewish views, there were Jews among his circle of friends and colleagues with whom he held close relationships throughout his life.

In 1850, Wagner published the *Das Judentum in der Musik* translated in English as *Judaism in Music.*[236] Wagner's argument was unusual and new, and as a leading composer, he felt only he could make such an argument. Wagner began his argument against Jews from the standpoint of art, especially music, attempting to explain why in his opinion, there were no truly great Jewish composers. He traces the root cause to the music found in Jewish religious services. In doing so, he immediately points to their religion, not just their culture and ethnicity, as a source of what is wrong with the Jews and what defines them as separate from German society, which for Wagner is a Christian society.

Who has not had occasion to convince himself of the travesty
of a divine service of song, presented in a real Folk-syna-
gogue? Who has not been seized with a feeling of the greatest
revulsion, of horror mingled with the absurd, at hearing that
sense-and-sound confounding gurgle, jodel and cackle, which
no intentional caricature can make more repugnant than as
offered here in full, in naive seriousness?[237]

Wagner however, goes on to discuss more than music, emphasizing
Jewish financial power in German society, and a supposed Jewish dominance of the business of art, something which the struggling and failed
artist Hitler would have related to.

According to the present constitution of this world, the Jew
in truth is already more than emancipate: he rules, and will
rule, so long as Money remains the power before which all
our doings and our dealings lose their force. That the historical adversity of the Jews and the rapacious rawness of
Christian-German potentates have brought this power within
the hands of Israel's sons—this needs no argument of ours to
prove.... that this has also brought the public Art-taste of our
time between the busy fingers of the Jew ... What their thralls
had toiled and moiled to pay the liege-lords of the Roman and
the Medieval world, to-day is turned to money by the Jew ...
What the heroes of the arts, with untold strain consuming lief
and life, have wrested from the art-fiend of two millennia of
misery, to-day the Jew converts into an art-bazaar.[238]

Wagner describes Jews as controllers of the business world. He
believed art should never be created for monetary profit. A mon-
ey-oriented society was killing the real arts, including Wagner's art, he
believed, and he criticized Jews who were merchants and business people. Wagner said in another work, "... whilst if the Jew comes tinkling
with his bell of paper, it throws its savings at his feet, and makes him
in one night a millionaire."[239] He believed Jews were taking money from
Germans. Hitler described Jews' business as "robbery." Wagner said in
Know Thyself,

If gold here figures as the demon strangling manhood's
innocence, our greatest poet shows at last the goblin's
game of paper money. The Nibelung's fateful ring become

a pocket-book, might well complete the eerie picture of the
spectral world-controller. By the advocates of our Progressive
Civilisation this rulership is indeed regarded as a spiritual,
nay, a moral power; for vanished Faith is now replaced by
"Credit." ...[240]

Judaism in Music emphasizes the other-ness of Jewish traits in
regards to their appearance, speech, language, and culture.[241] Wagner
argued that Jews were not good for music because their language is not
German, and therefore they could not speak German from their hearts.
Jewish artists, he said, are therefore superficial and deceptive.

The first thing that strikes our ear as quite outlandish and
unpleasant, in the Jew's production of the voice-sounds, is a
creaking, squeaking, buzzing snuffle.... Now, if the aforesaid
qualities of his dialect make the Jew almost incapable of giving artistic enunciation to his feelings and beholdings through
talk, for such an enunciation through *song* his aptitude must
needs be infinitely smaller. Song is just Talk aroused to highest passion: Music is the speech of Passion.

When this had once been spoken out, there was nothing left
but to babble after; and indeed with quite distressing accuracy
and deceptive likeness, just as parrots reel off human words
and phrases, but also with just as little real feeling and expression as these foolish birds....[242]

Wagner compared the well-known Jewish composer Felix Mendelssohn (1809–1847) to German composers such as Beethoven and
Mozart,[243] and criticized his music, after he died.

Whereas Beethoven, the last in the chain of our true
music-heroes, strove with highest longing, and wonder-work-
ing faculty, for the clearest, certainest Expression of an
unsayable Content through a sharp-cut, plastic shaping of his
tone-pictures: Mendelssohn, on the contrary, reduces these
achievements to vague, fantastic shadow-forms, midst whose
indefinite shimmer our freakish fancy is indeed aroused, but
our inner, purely-human yearning for distinct artistic sight is
hardly touched with even the merest hope of a fulfillment.[244]

Wagner explained what makes true art, and shared his philosophy of art and music, which he thought that a Jew could not possibly be capable of expressing:

> The Jews could never take possession of this art, until *that* was to be exposed in it which they now demonstrably have brought to light—its inner incapacity for life. So long as the separate art of Music had a real organic life-need in it, down to the epochs of Mozart and Beethoven, there was nowhere to be found a Jew composer: it was impossible for an element entirely foreign to that living organism to take part in the formative stages of that life. Only when a body's inner death is manifest, do outside elements win the power of lodgment in it—yet merely to destroy it....[245]

Wagner mentions a Jewish poet, Heinrich Heine, whom he insists "duped himself into a poet, and was rewarded by his versified lies being set to music by our own composers.—He was the conscience of Judaism, just as Judaism is the evil conscience of our modern Civilisation."[246]

In the last phrase of *Judaism in Music*, Wagner concludes "But bethink ye, that one only thing can redeem you from the burden of your curse: the redemption of Ahasuerus—*Going under!*"[247] This sentence is ambiguous. It could refer to the medieval legend of the wandering Jew, who in some versions of the legend was called Ahasuerus. The legend describes a Jew who slapped and taunted Jesus on his way to his crucifixion and was cursed to wander the earth as punishment. In at least one version of the legend, Ahasuerus is baptized and lives out his life as a hermit. It can be interpreted that Wagner is saying that the only thing that can save Jews is to convert, with the phrase "going under" meaning to go under water in the act of baptism. Mendelssohn was born to a Jewish family; though raised without practicing any religion, he was baptized as a Reform Christian at the age of 7.[248]

The phrase could also be interpreted as referring to the Persian king who ordered the massacre of the Jews in the Old Testament in the book of Esther.

> It was written in the name of King Ahasuerus and sealed with the king's signet ring. Letters were sent by couriers to all the king's provinces with instruction to destroy, to kill, and to annihilate all Jews, young and old, women and children, in

> one day, the thirteenth day of the twelfth month, which is the
> month of Adar, and to plunder their goods.[249]

In this case, "going under" means to the destruction and annihilation of Jews, and could have served as an inspiration for the Holocaust.[250]

Judaism in Music had a small printing run, only about 1,500–2,000 copies, was not widely disseminated, and rarely reprinted later, though it was reprinted during the Nazi regime. Although it is unknown for certain if Hitler read it earlier, considering what a great fan he was of Wagner, it is likely he did. Hitler surely at least knew of it at the time it was reprinted. Despite its small circulation, some scholars consider it to be a seminal document in the beginnings of publicly expressed anti-Semitism in Germany.

[3] Victory of the Idea of Creative Work

The main passage of *Mein Kampf* concerning the Hook-Cross emphasizes that it symbolized "the victory of the idea of creative work, which as such always has been and always will be anti-Semitic." The phrase "creative work" recalls the image of Wagner's creativity and his "total works of art." Wagner created great works of art centered on the German spirit. Operas, like any art, are open to interpretation by viewers, and Hitler might have interpreted that Wagner's operas were great creative works meant to carry a message of anti-Semitism.

One of the key words for Hitler is "work" (*Arbeit*). In his speech "Why We Are Anti-Semites" delivered on August 13, 1920, Hitler begins by defining three different levels of "work." The first is "an effect of a simple instinct of self-preservation" which he says is also seen in animals. The second stage of work is "one from pure egoism." And the third is the "work out of ethical sense of duty, where an individual does not work because he is forced to it." This last one is related to Hitler's idea of a "deep spiritual life."[251] Hitler twice praised Wagner's music as a great example of work in the speech.

> The moment the small, powerless stateless began to unite into
> one state, then also one German art, proud of itself, began to
> grow. The works of Richard Wagner appeared in the period
> when shame and powerlessness were replaced by a unified,
> great German Reich.[252]

Our theater, the places which a Richard Wagner wanted once to have darkened to create the highest degree of consecration and seriousness, in which he wanted to perform works which it would be shameful to call shows, so he named them "consecration plays"; the place where there should be nothing else but the highest elevation, a detachment of the individual from all the grief and misery, but also from all the rot which surrounds us in life, to lift the individual into a purer air.[253]

Wagner was also known for supporting the Aryan superiority of the German race, though *Judaism in Music* did not discuss this aspect directly. His *Hero-dom and Christendom* claimed the superiority of the white race, Aryan qualities, and German nationalism.

We cannot withhold our acknowledgment that the human family consists of irredeemably disparate races, whereof the noble could rule the ignoble, yet never raise them to their level by commixture, but simply sink to theirs. Indeed this one relation might suffice to explain our fall....

Whilst yellow races have viewed themselves as sprung from monkeys, the white traced back their origin to gods, and deemed themselves marked out for rulership. It has been made quite clear that we should have no History of Man at all, had there been no movements, creations, and achievements of the white man....

Like Herakles and Siegfried, they were conscious of divine descent: a lie to them was inconceivable, and a free man meant a truthful man. Nowhere in history do the root qualities of the Aryan race show forth more plainly than in the contact of the last pure-bred Germanic branches with the falling Roman world.[254]

It certainly may be right to charge this purblind dullness of our public spirit to the vitiation of our blood—not only by departure from the natural food of man, but above all by the tainting of the hero-blood of the noblest races with that of former cannibals now trained to be the business agents of Society.[255]

[4] Wagner and Eastern Religions

One of the reasons for Hitler's choice of the swastika symbol may have also been that the symbol is deeply related to Buddhism and Hinduism, the two religions that Wagner respected in addition to Christianity. Wagner had been interested in Eastern philosophy from when he first met Schopenhauer in 1845. The influence of Eastern thought is evident in *Parsifal* as well as Wagner's unfinished work, *Die Sieger*. Wagner explained in *Religion and Art*

> If we follow up that phase in the evolution of the human race which we call the Historic, as based on sure tradition, it is easier to comprehend why the religions arising in course of this period fell deeper and deeper in their inward spirit, the longer was their outward rule. The two sublimest of religions, Brahminism with its offshoot Buddhism, and Christianity, teach alienation from the world and its passions, thus steering straight against the flow of the world-tide without being able in truth to stem it.[256]

Wagner's understanding of Christianity is rooted in the Reformers, particularly Martin Luther. Hitler meanwhile, may have seen the swastika symbol as an "Aryan" bridge connecting Buddhism and Christianity, which following Aryan invasion theory, provided proof that superior white Aryans had brought more sophisticated culture with them to various parts of Asia. As Hitler wrote, "You will find this cross as a Hakenkreuz as far as India and Japan, carved in the temple pillars. It is the Hakenkreuz, which was once a sign of established communities of Aryan Culture."[257]

Even when Hitler recognized the swastika as a symbol used in the East, he still saw it as a type of Aryan cross that must have come from somewhere else rather than as a symbol that had been used coincidentally in different religions and cultures in different parts of the world at different times. The existence and influence of Aryan invasion theory prevented Hitler from recognizing and understanding the swastika as a native Eastern religious symbol.

When Hitler said, "Whoever wants to understand National Socialist Germany must know Wagner," it was not an exaggeration. If one knows Wagner, one will discover reflected in the creative works of his music an important source of Hitler's theories of a German Aryan race, and anti-Semitism. Wagner's operas planted the seeds for Hitler's own creative theatrical propaganda, a fusion of the power of religion, art, and politics, of which the Hakenkreuz-swastika was a potent visual and symbolic central element. Hitler's creative artwork was the sensational Hakenkreuz, created by adopting the lucky charm symbol of the swastika from the East instilled with a new resignification combining "Aryan" superiority, German Christianity, and anti-Semitism.

Luther, Wagner, and Hitler

The strength and basis of Hitler's anti-Semitism evolved from a larger European anti-Semitism that in Germany included the influence of Luther and Wagner. It did not always include the idea of race, and the concept of a superior Aryan master race was not only associated with anti-Semitism. Martin Luther's anti-Semitism had religious roots, based on a presumed superiority of Christianity above all other religions. In that framework, Jews, as the other, become a natural enemy. Richard Wagner's anti-Semitism had racial roots stemming from ideas of a mythical Germanic superiority. Both Luther and Wagner, and later Hitler, all saw their struggles against the Jews and other races as conflicts of righteous justice. These conflicts were central to all their created dramas, both on stage and in real life, the motivation that drove them in all their creative works. Waging these struggles against an "other" they defined as evil, conferred a sense of the heroic to their actions. Waging them in the name of Christianity highlighted the righteous justice of their causes, and the prominence of the cross-flag of Hitler, who imagined himself as Luther and Wagner's successor, visually encapsulated that struggle. Though the symbol itself originated in Eastern religions, Hitler in many ways saw his version of the swastika as a type of Christian cross, resignified as a symbol of German superiority and anti-Semitism.

Political Symbol vs. Religious and Spiritual Symbol

Hitler chose to use the symbol with his new interpretation and for his own political purpose. The swastika did not choose Hitler. The swastika has been chosen by many cultures and religions as the symbol of the sun, good fortune, and auspiciousness, and billions of people have received the benefit over three thousand years including those who follow Buddhism, Jainism, and Hinduism. The swastika is not responsible for Hitler's actions. The swastika is a symbol, whose meaning lies in what others pour into it. Hitler's actions were his own responsibility. The sacred swastika was hijacked, falsely represented, and badly damaged with a political purpose by Hitler. This desecration continues now by racist hate groups and individuals, causing the broader meaning of the swastika to not be recognized and appreciated in the West at present.

SIX

Hitler's Symbol Is a Hakenkreuz, Not a Swastika

Difference between "Swastika" and "Hakenkreuz"

"Swastika" in English has been used since before the time of Hitler as a general term to describe the swastika symbol, while "Hakenkreuz" is a specific term referring to the Nazi Germany emblem. Therefore, most English dictionaries use the common, general word "swastika" to explain the Hakenkreuz, which, for example, can be found defined as "The Nazi swastika,"[258] "the swastika used as a symbol of German anti-Semitism or of Nazi Germany,"[259] and the "proper German name for the Nazi swastika."[260]

Swastika as a general term in English includes:

... and more.

Hakenkreuz (Hook-Cross) specifically means:

 and

The Hakenkreuz, because of its shape, can be seen as a type of swastika. The word "swastika" refers to many various kinds of swastikas, not only Hitler's Hakenkreuz. However, the present English language does not recognize "swastika" as a general term, but only Hitler's Hakenkreuz.

Yet from Hitler's viewpoint, the Hakenkreuz was not just a swastika, but actually one of the many varieties of crosses that have existed throughout history:

$$† + ⸸ T ‡ ⸭ ⅏ + X ⸸$$

Hitler's Hakenkreuz should be explained as a kind of cross, based upon Hitler's own concept of his symbol as expressed through the name he assigned to it, the Hook-Cross. The Christian theology prevalent in Germany at the time, drawn from Luther, and an ideology of German superiority, drawn from Wagner, as well as the image itself, suggests that seeing the Nazi emblem as a "Hook-Cross" is a more apt understanding than continuing to think of it as the "swastika" symbol of luck prevalent in the East.

From that perspective, the definitions of the Hakenkreuz listed above should be changed more accurately to "The Nazi *cross*," "the *cross* used as a symbol of German anti-Semitism or of Nazi Germany," or the "proper German name for the Nazi *cross*."

Another example illustrating Hitler's clear view of the Hakenkreuz as a cross symbol is the name of the "German Cross," or *Deutsches Kreuz* in German, an award medal which was established by Hitler in 1941 (Fig. 101). The medal's design features Hitler's Hakenkreuz prominently in its center surrounded by a laurel wreath and what appear to be sunrays. The medal was created as an intermediate award between the Iron Cross, First Class, and the Knight's Cross. The Gold Laurel Wreath version was awarded "for outstanding bravery" and the Silver "for special achievements in troop leadership."[261] The fact that Hitler chose to use the word "cross" in the medal's name is further evidence that Hitler saw the symbol as a type of cross. Furthermore, Hitler often combined the Hakenkreuz symbol with that of the cross, for example in some of the Iron Cross medals, including the Mother's Cross, and in other visual imagery (Figs. 102–105). The flag of German Christians (*Deutsche Christen Flagge*), the German Protestants who embraced and supported the Nazi ideology, combined the signs of the Crucifixion Cross and Hitler's Hook-Cross.

101. German Cross (1941).

102. Nazi Iron Cross (1939).

103. German battle flag.

104. German Mother's Cross.

105. German Christian flag.

Hitler Called It "Hakenkreuz"

Hitler could have called the symbol a "swastika" or "swastica," which was what many people in Germany called the symbol at that time, but he instead made the deliberate choice to use the word "Hakenkreuz." He was aware of its history as an Eastern symbol, as he himself described the symbol when introducing the Hakenkreuz flag in 1920.

Hitler's choice is perhaps an example of how German nationalism was reflected in the German language of that era. "Swastika" is clearly a Sanskrit word from India, while "Hakenkreuz" is clearly a German term that emphasizes that the symbol was not foreign but Germany's own. Considering the goals for the nation that Hitler described in *Mein Kampf*, the new symbol needed to be called "Hakenkreuz." It was a "new" symbol, with an Aryan German word to describe it for what was supposed to be a new glory-era revival for Germany—the Third Reich. Yet through its clear visual similarity to the Eastern swastika, it simultaneously provided a connection to an ancient world history myth in which Germans, through the racially predetermined "Aryan" birthright, could rule over and slaughter others at will. As a variation of a cross, the symbol also implied a link to a divine mandate to do the same. As a cross, it could be neatly swapped in for the crucifix at German Christian churches to further Hitler's cult of the state, bridging his cult with the already existing churches. When German people hear the word "Hakenkreuz," they could immediately understand the symbol as a kind of cross, because the word is built into the term. Most English-speaking people on the other hand, when they hear the word "swastika," do not associate the symbol with a cross at all because the word used to describe it has nothing to do with a cross.

Hitler always used the term "Hakenkreuz," which literally translates to "Hook-Cross," to refer to his symbol. The word "Hakenkreuz" was a German word used to refer to the swastika shape as a heraldic symbol according to the 1877 edition of the comprehensive German dictionary *Deutsches Worterbuch*.[262] The word "swastika" or any similar variants do not appear in this dictionary, because it was not commonly known in Germany at that time. It did not become well known until after Schliemann's excavations of Troy in the late 1870s and Muller's language theory later popularized it.

Muller, in a letter written to Schliemann, advocated against using the word "swastika" to describe any swastikas not found in India because he did not want the public to see it as a symbol originating in India. Muller wrote:

> I do not like the use of the word *svastika* outside of India. It is a word of Indian origin and has its history and definite meaning in India...Another objection to the promiscuous use of the word *Svastika* is, that *svastika* in Sanskrit does not mean the Hakenkreuz, *crux ansata*, in general, but only the cross with the hooks pointing to the right, 卐,while the cross with the hooks pointing to the left, 卍, is called Sauvastika... The occurrence of such crosses may not point to a common origin, but if they are once called *Svastika* the *vulgus profanum* will at once jump to the conclusion that they all come from India, and it will take some time to weed out such prejudice.[263]

Muller clearly makes a distinction between two versions of the symbol assigning them two different words, "svastika" (swastika) and "sauvastika," though in Sanskrit there is actually only the word "svastika."

The symbol is also described as a Hakenkreuz in the *Secret of the Runes*, an influential occultist book published in 1908 by the Austrian mystic Guido von List. The book lists the symbol in an illustrated compilation of ancient German heraldic symbols.[264]

However, by the time Hitler was a young man in the early 1900s, the word "swastika" was often used as a borrowed word in the German language to refer to the Eastern symbol, which was by then quite popular in Europe as a lucky symbol. It is therefore reasonable to assume Hitler was aware of the word's existence, yet he deliberately chose the other term, Hakenkreuz, to refer to his version of the symbol, which he infused with new meanings.

Hitler was aware of the swastika symbol, and was also aware of its association with the term "Aryan," at least as it was understood in Germany at that time. During the speech Hitler repeatedly referred to the symbol as a Hakenkreuz, or just a "kreuz" (cross). This appears to be Hitler's first known use of the word "Hakenkreuz." He said, "You will find this cross as a Hakenkreuz as far as India and Japan, carved in the temple pillars. It is the Hakenkreuz, which was once a sign of established communities of Aryan Culture."[265]

The second volume of *Mein Kampf,* published in 1926 in the original German. repeatedly uses the word "Hakenkreuz" to refer to Hitler's symbol. The first quotation below describes how the flag's design was selected. The second quotation describes how the symbol represented Hitler's political vision at that time and the meanings that he assigned to it. The following quotations are in both German and English to show what Hitler said in the original and how it was later translated into English.[266]

(1) *Ich selbst trat immer für die Beibehaltung der alten Farben ein, nicht nur weil sie mir als Soldat das Heiligste sind, das ich kenne, sondern weil sie auch in ihrer ästhetischen Wirkung meinem Gefühl weitaus am meisten entsprechen. Dennoch mußte ich die zahllosen Entwürfe, die damals aus den Kreisen der jungen Bewegung einliefen, und die meistens das **Hakenkreuz** in die alte Fahne hineingezeichnet hatten, ausnahmslos ablehnen. Ich selbst—als Führer—wollte nicht sofort mit meinem eigenen Entwurf an die Öffentlichkeit treten, da es ja möglich war, daß ein anderer einen ebenso guten oder vielleicht auch besseren bringen würde. Tatsächlich hat ein Zahnarzt aus Starnberg auch einen gar nicht schlechten Entwurf geliefert, der übrigens dem meinem ziemlich nahekam, nur den einen Fehler hatte, daß das **Hakenkreuz** mit gebogenen Haken in eine weiße Scheibe hineinkomponiert war.*

I myself always came out for the retention of the old colors, not only because as a soldier they are to me the holiest thing I know, but because also in their esthetic effect they are by far the most compatible with my feeling. Nevertheless, I was obliged to reject without exception the numerous designs which poured in from the circles of the young movement, and which for the most part had drawn the **swastika** into the old flag. I myself—as Leader—did not want to come out publicly at once with my own design, since after all it was possible that another should produce one just as good or perhaps even better. Actually, a dentist from Starnberg did deliver a design that was not bad at all, and, incidentally, was quite close to my own, having only the one fault that a **swastika** with curved legs was composed into a white disk.

(2) *Als nationale Sozialisten sehen wir in unserer Flagge unser Programm. Im Rot sehen wir den sozialen Gedanken der Bewegung, im Weiß den nationalsozialistischen, im **Hakenkreuz** die Mission des*

Kampfes für den Sieg des arischen Menschen und zugleich mit ihm
auch den Sieg des Gedankens der schaffenden Arbeit, die selbst ewig
antisemitisch war und antisemitisch sein wird.

As National Socialists, we see our program in our flag. In red
we see the social idea of the movement, in white the nationalistic idea, in the **swastika** the mission of the struggle for the
victory of the Aryan man, and, by the same token, the victory
of the idea of creative work, which as such always has been
and always will be anti-Semitic.

Many in the West believe that Hitler invented the swastika symbol.
He didn't. Many also believe he invented the word "swastika" to describe
it. He didn't do that either. But he did consciously use a different German
word, "Hakenkreuz," and that is more significant, because in the use of
that word we can see how Hitler saw the symbol and the way he manip-
ulated its original Eastern meanings to suit his own vision, which was
antithetical to those original meanings.

Definition of "Hakenkreuz"

According to *Webster's New Collegiate Dictionary* (1973), the word
"Hakenkreuz" is defined as:

> ha·ken·kreuz *n*. often cap [G, fr. *haken* hook + *kreuz* cross]:
> the swastika used as a symbol of anti-Semitism or of Nazi
> Germany.

It consists of two words combined: *haken* meaning "hook, bent,
curve" and; *kreuz* meaning "cross." So, the word literally means "hook-
cross," "bent-cross," or "curve-cross."

Online Etymology Dictionary[267] describes the Hakenkreuz as a proper
German name for the swastika first used by the Nazis in 1931. The year
1931 in this definition probably originates in the *Oxford English Dictionary*, but Hitler and the National Socialist Party used the Hakenkreuz
flag for the first time in the summer of 1920 according to *Mein Kampf.*[268]
In the *Oxford English Dictionary (Second Edition)*, published in 1989 by
Clarendon Press, the entry for "Hakenkreuz" says:

> **Hakenkreuz, hakenkreuz** [Ger.] The Nazi swastika. Also *attrib.*
> **1931** *Times* 23 Dec. 7/4 A large Nazi Hakenkreuz flag, 'which can be seen for miles', flies from the tallest chimney. **1935** C. ISHERWOOD Mr. *Norris changes Trains* xi. 165 Hitler's negotiations with the Right had broken down; the Hakenkreuz was even flirting mildly with the Hammer and Sickle. **1966** 'M. ALBRAND' Door fell Shut xvi. 115 His eyes fell on a large hakenkreuz. To come upon the Nazi insignia so unexpectedly made Bronsky feel slightly sick. **1972** Oxford Times 28 July 9 Perhaps he [sc. Hitler] hoped the Hakenkreuz would bring bad luck to his enemies.

According to this entry, the word "Hakenkreuz" used as an English term first appeared in the *London Times* in 1931 as the name of the Nazi flag. It was used as a proper noun, not a common noun.

There is an earlier reference in the *New York Times* that disproves the O.E.D.s' reference to 1931 as the first printed appearance of the word "Hakenkreuz" as a borrowed word in English. A *New York Times* article dated December 2, 1923, found in the *New York Times* archives uses of the word "Hakenkreuz" to describe the Nazi emblem. This is the earliest printed English-language reference to the Hakenkreuz in the *New York Times*. The story quotes a witness describing the scene inside the Munich beer hall where Hitler and the National Socialists announced their attempted coup to take over the government a month earlier: "We see a couple of uniforms, a Hakenkreuz sash and Hitler!"[269] There are no appearances in the *New York Times* prior to this story. Following it, several articles appear which use the word to refer to the Nazi symbol or the Nazi flag containing the symbol until 1933. Only once, in 1932, the *Times* used the word "swastika" to refer to the Nazi symbol.[270]

The *New York Times* also mentions the "Hakenkreuz Banner" as the name of the Nazi Party newspaper in articles from 1933 and 1934. Although the Nazi paper was published in German, the *Times* kept the term "Hakenkreuz" and did not use the word "swastika" in these articles, or the term "hooked cross" for that matter.

A story published March 19, 1933, in the *New York Times*, appears under the title "Hooked Cross an Old Symbol, From India the Swastika Made its Way to Germany." The *New York Times* would have been more accurate if it were written instead: "Swastika an Old Symbol from India Made Its Way to Germany as the Hooked Cross."

The piece describes the history of the symbol and uses the terms "hooked cross" and "swastika" as if they are interchangeable. The lead says:

> Under a decree signed by President von Hindenburg all German public buildings fly side by side, the black-and-white-and-red flag of Imperial Germany and the Nazi banner with the swastika or hooked cross. By another decree the black and gold-and-red republican colors were banished from the German war flag.[271]

Right there in the opening, the sentence's syntax which puts the word "swastika" first before the phrase "or hooked cross" communicates to the reader that the word "swastika" is the primary word that should be used to refer to the symbol in English, while also equating it to the second term "hooked cross." The article then continues to use the term "swastika" exclusively to refer to both Hitler's symbol and all other swastikas.

Besides its headline, the story also contains another, more glaring inaccuracy. It says "Hitler first foisted the swastika on Germany ten years ago, interpreting it as a sign of youth, of daring and of Germanism." This is true. However, the writer continues in the next sentence to state that the swastika "was used as a symbol in ancient Germany to represent the supremacy of the Aryan, or Nordic, race over others, a thought underlying the Nazi movement." This claim, stated as fact, is incorrect and although the author gives no attribution, is obviously sourced from popular notions of Aryan invasion theory. But there is no mention of Muller, Burnouf, or anything to indicate this is a scholarly theory rather than a universally accepted fact, which is what the author implies by not offering any attribution.

While the writer correctly described the swastika symbol's ubiquitous presence in many ancient cultures around the globe, there is no mention of the symbol's positive meanings of good luck and good fortune. The story describes it as a "mystic symbol" of uncertain origin with varied meanings including that of fire, water, rains, a rotating sun, or a flash of lightening. The only attribution for these meanings are "one authority" and "several scholars," all anonymous, as is the story's author.

Perhaps it is this article that initiated the shift toward using the word "swastika" instead of "Hakenkreuz" in English-language media and in common usage to describe Hitler's symbol. After this story appeared, the *New York Times* primarily used the term "swastika" to refer to Hitler's symbol rather than Hakenkreuz. The story, by drawing a false association between the meaning of Hitler's symbol with the meaning of the ancient symbol and also by equating the words "Hooked Cross" and "Swastika," helped to popularize an incorrect image and desecrated the original meaning of the ancient symbol.

"Swastika" and "Hakenkreuz" in Dictionaries

A *New English Dictionary on Historical Principles* published in 1884, includes an entry for "swastika" (also svastika, swastica), but no entry for "Hakenkreuz." The "swastika" entry says it "is known as fylfot or gammadion" but does not mention the word "Hakenkreuz." This is because the Hakenkreuz as a borrowed formal noun did not yet exist in English.

Below are examples of how the word "swastika" was used in English before WWII from the *Oxford English Dictionary (Second Edition)* in 1989.

> **1871** ALABASRTER *Wheel of Law* 249 On the great toe is the Trisul. On each side of the others a Swastika. **1882** E.C. ROBERTSON in *Proc. Berw. Nat. Club* IX. No. 3. 516 In Japan, the cross-like symbol of the sun, the Swastica, is put on coffins. **1895** *Reliquary* Oct. 252 The use of the Swastica cross in medieval times. **1904** *Times* 27 Aug. 10/3 [In Tibet] a few white, straitened hovels in tiers ... On the door of each is a kicking swastika in white, and over it a rude daub of ball and crescent.

This OED entry reveals that the word "swastika" was used in English prior to WWII to mean the positive sacred swastika. There are no references to anything having to do with hate, evil, and racism. The original meaning of the swastika in the East and the words that described it existed well before Hitler's time.

During Hitler's rise to power, "Hakenkreuz" became an English word borrowed from German and used to mean the Nazi emblem, though later, after the *New York Times* 1933 article, the word disappeared from many dictionaries and newspapers. The word "swastika" eventually took the place of the word "Hakenkreuz." The original meaning of the swastika then disappeared from many popular dictionaries, including web dictionaries which many people use nowadays. The online *Longman Dictionary of Contemporary English*, for example, has only this definition for the word "swastika": "a sign consisting of a cross with each end bent at 90 degrees, used as a sign for the Nazi Party in Germany."[272] The *Webster's New World Portable Large Print Dictionary*, published in 1992, defines the swastika as a "cross with bent arms: Nazi emblem." Although this entry contains a two-part definition, the first merely describes the symbol's shape absent of meaning, while the second part offers a single meaning, that of Hitler's symbol. The entry for swastika in the *New American Webster Handy College Dictionary Fourth Edition* says simply: "a form of cross adopted as the emblem of the Nazi Party." The dictionary was published in 2006 and boasts on its cover of "more than 16 million copies in print!"

As discussed previously, *Webster's New Collegiate Dictionary*, published in 1973, makes a clear distinction between the Hakenkreuz and swastika with two separate entries for the different words. The "swastika" entry does not include the meaning of Hitler's swastika.

> **ha·ken·kreuz** *n. often cap* [G, fr. *haken* hook + *kreuz* cross]: the swastika used as a symbol of German anti-Semitism or of Nazi Germany.

> **swas·ti·ka** *n* [Skt *svastika*, fr. *svasti* welfare, fr. *su-* well + *asti* he is; akin to OE *is*; fr. Its being regarded as a good luck symbol]: a symbol or ornament in the form of a Greek cross with the ends of the arms extended at right angles all in the same rotary direction.

Most general English dictionaries from WWII onward, other than the OED, include two meanings for the swastika. For example, the *1993 Merriam-Webster's Collegiate Dictionary, 10th Edition*, contains two meanings in the entry for swastika. There is no Hakenkreuz entry. They are:

> **swas·ti·ka** *n* [Skt *svastika*, fr. *svasti* well-being, fr. su- well + as- to be; akin to Skt *asti* he is, OE *is*; fr. its being regarded as a good luck symbol] (1871) 1: a symbol or ornament in the form

of a Greek cross with the ends of the arms extended at right angles all in the same rotary direction 2: a swastika used as a symbol of anti-Semitism or of Nazism.

Interestingly, the entries in both versions that describe the non-Nazi definition attribute the origins of the word to Sanskrit. Yet they describe the symbol as a "Greek cross" with no mention of it as an Eastern symbol associated with Eastern religions. Perhaps this is a remnant of the Euro-centric Indo-European language myth.

The intention of *Webster's New Collegiate Dictionary* at one point seems to have been to make a distinction between the Hakenkreuz and swastika, as both were treated as two separate words in 1973. However, when more recent English dictionaries are consulted, such as the 1993 version of Webster's, most do not list the word "Hakenkreuz." Instead, the "swastika" entry lists two meanings with no mention of the word "Hakenkreuz." Some small dictionaries list only the meaning of Hitler's swastika and its use as an anti-Semitism symbol, with no mention of the positive Eastern meanings of the swastika.

Thomas Wilson's *Swastika: The Earliest Known Symbol and Its Migrations* in 1894, although not a dictionary, is a comprehensive catalog of the swastika symbol's meanings around the world prior to Hitler. It does not mention the word "Hakenkreuz," though it refers to fylfot, gammadion, thor's hammer, Croix gammee, svastika and *manji* as different words used for the swastika symbol around the world.

When German people use the word "Hakenkreuz," it means Hitler's Nazi emblem, not the Eastern symbols of Hinduism, Buddhism, and Jainism. The Eastern symbol is called a swastika. It is the same way in Japan; as explained in the previous chapters, "Hakenkreuz" in Japanese is called "haakenkuroitsu" or "kagi-juji," and "swastika" is called "manji." Below are examples of the words used in other European countries, and Japan to describe the Hakenkreuz and Swastika:

In German, Hakenkreuz vs. Swastika;
in French, croix gammée vs. Svastika, swastika;
in Italian, croce uncinata vs. svastica;
in Spanish, cruz gamada vs. esvástica;
in Dutch, Hakenkruis vs. swastika;
in Swedish, Hakkros vs. svastika;
and in Japanese, haakenkuroitsu, kagi-juji vs. *manji*.

In contrast with English, each of these examples uses the word "cross" in the word to represent Hitler's symbol. In French and Spanish, "Hakenkreuz" is translated as "cross with gamma." Gamma (Γ) is the third letter of Greek alphabet. The French word "croix" means "cross," and "gammée"means "gamma." The Spanish word "cruz" means "cross," and "gamada" means "gamma." In Italian, "croce" means "cross," and "uncinata" means "hook sedge" which is a genus of flowering plants of the family Cyperaceae. Therefore, "Hakenkreuz" is translated as "a cross-like hook-sedge." In Dutch, "haken" means "hook," and "kruis" means "cross." In Swedish, "Hak" means "hook," and "kros" means "cross." "Hakenkreuz" is translated as "hook-cross." In Japanese, "Hākenkuroitsu" is a transliteration of "Hakenkreuz." It is also translated into Japanese as "Kagi-juji." The Japanese term "kagi" means "hook," and "juji' means "cross." The swastika in contrast is called a "manji," which means "word of ten thousand (all) virtues."

Because English translators used the term "swastika" to describe the Hakenkreuz, there is now only one word in English to express the two separate meanings of Hitler's swastika and the Eastern swastika. Younger generations born after the war have no knowledge or memory of the swastika's earlier history and popular history around the world as a positive, lucky symbol. Nowadays, the word "swastika" is only known as a taboo word in English.

What could have been the benefit from translating "Hakenkreuz" into "swastika"? It might have been that the swastika could hide and shield the cross. Perhaps America and England wanted to prevent their citizens from an image that their enemy, Nazi Germany, was fighting under a cross, which is a sacred symbol for Christianity, to prevent any feeling of affinity or sympathy. Emphasizing the otherness of Hitler's symbol, that it was a symbol of pure evil, may have been a way to demonize the enemy. This is speculation. However, visual propaganda was an important part of the Allied war effort, and was also used to demonize the Japanese—and Japanese Americans, so this is a possibility. What is certain is that the word "swastika" would not have become a taboo term if the English language had two separate words.

Translation Problems of "Hakenkreuz"

Volume 1 of *Mein Kampf* was written in 1925 and Volume 2 of *Mein Kampf* was published in 1926, while Hitler was in prison. By the end of the war, about 10 million copies of the book were sold and distributed in Germany, and also translated into various languages including English, Arabic, French, and Japanese. There are several English translations of *Mein Kampf.* In the original German texts by Adolf Hitler, the word "Hakenkreuz" appears eight times in Volume 2, Chapter 7, "The Struggle with the Red Front." Neither the words "swastika," "svastika," "swastica," nor any other variations are used in the original German *Mein Kampf* or in any other materials written by Hitler in German. However, all but one of the English translations that exist use the term "swastika" as a translation of "Hakenkreuz."

[1] Various English Translations of *Mein Kampf*

There are four major English translations that were done between 1933 and 1943. They are:

> Ralph Manheim Translation, published by Houghton Mifflin Company, Boston, MA in 1943. This is the most popular translation in English.

> Translation Committee (including John Chamberlain, Sidney B Fay and eight other translators), published by Reynal & Hitchcock, New York, NY in 1940.

> James Murphy Translation, published by Hutchison & Co., London in 1939.

> Edgar T. S. Dugdale Translation, published by Houghton Mifflin Company, Boston, MA in 1933. Title is "My Battle" in America, and "My Struggle" in UK. This is the first translation of *Mein Kampf* into English. It is an abridged version.

The following is a comparison of how the term "Hakenkreuz" was translated in each.[273]

> *Dennoch mußte ich die zahllosen Entwürfe, die damals aus den Kreisen der jungen Bewegung einliefen, und die meistens das **Hakenkreuz***

in die alte Fahne hineingezeichnet hatten, ausnahmslos ablehnen....
Tatsächlich hat ein Zahnarzt aus Starnberg auch einen gar nicht
schlechten Entwurf geliefert, der übrigens dem meinem ziemlich
nahekam, nur den einen Fehler hatte, daß das **Hakenkreuz** *mit gebo-*
genen Haken in eine weiße Scheibe hineinkomponiert war.

[Manheim's Translation]
Nevertheless, I was obliged to reject without exception the
numerous designs which poured in from the circles of the
young movement, and which for the most part had drawn
the **swastika** into the old flag ... Actually, a dentist from
Starnberg did deliver a design that was not bad at all, and,
incidentally, was quite close to my own, having only the one
fault that a **swastika** with curved legs was composed into a
white disk.

[Chamberlain and Fay's Translation]
Yet, I had to reject, without exception, the numerous designs
that in those days were handed in by the circles of the young
movement and that mostly had placed the **swastika** on the
old flag.... In fact, a dentist from Starnberg produced a design
that was not bad at all, and besides that approached my own
design very closely, except that it had the one mistake that the
swastika was composed on a white circle with curved hooks.

[Murphy's Translation]
Accordingly I had to discard all the innumerable suggestions
and designs which had been proposed for the new movement
among which were many that had incorporated the **swastika**
into the old colours.... As a matter of fact, a dental surgeon
from Starnberg submitted a good design very similar to mine,
with only one mistake, in that his **swastika** with curved cor-
ners was set upon a white background.

(In Dugdale's translation this section was omitted and not
translated.)

Ich selbst hatte unterdes nach unzähligen Versuchen eine endgültige
Form niedergelegt; eine Fahne aus roten Grundtuch mit einer weißen
Scheibe und in deren Mitte ein schwarzes **Hakenkreuz.** *Nach langen*
Versuchen fand ich auch ein bestimmtes Verhältnis zwischen der
Größe der Fahne und der Größe der weißen scheibe sowie der Form
und Stärke des **Hakenkreuzes.**

[Manheim's Translation]
I myself, meanwhile, after innumerable attempts, had laid down a final form; a flag with a red background, a white disk, and a black **swastika** in the middle. After long trials I also found a definite proportion between the size of the flag and the size of the white disk, as well as the shape and thickness of the **swastika**. And this remained final.

[Chamberlain and Fay's Translation]
Meanwhile, I myself, after innumerable attempts, had put down a final form: a flag with a background of red with a white circle, and in its center, a black **swastika**. And this then was kept.

[Murphy's Translation]
After innumerable trials I decided upon a final form—a flag of red material with a white disc bearing in its centre a black **swastika**. After many trials I obtained the correct proportions between the dimensions of the flag and of the white central disc, as well as that of the **swastika**. And this is how it has remained ever since.

[Dugdale's Translation]
I myself was always for keeping the old colours. After innumerable trials I settled upon a final form: a flag having a red ground with a white disc in it bearing on its centre a black **hooked cross**. After much searching I decided on the proper portions between the size of the flag and that of the white disc and the form and thickness of the **cross**; and it has remained so ever since.

*Und dabei ist es dann geblieben. In gleichem Sinne wurden nun sofort Armbinden für die Ordnungsmannschaften in Auftrag gegeben, und zwar eine rote Binde, auf der sich ebenfalls die weiße Scheibe mit schwarzem **Hakenkreuz** befindet. Auch das Parteiabzeichen wurde nach gleichen Richtlinien entworfen: eine weiße Scheibe auf rotem Felde und in der Mitte das **Hakenkreuz**. Ein Münchner Goldschmied, Füß, lieferte den ersten verwendbaren und dann auch beibehaltenen Entwurf.*

[Manheim's Translation]
Along the same lines arm-bands were immediately ordered for the monitor detachments, a red band, likewise with the white disk and black **swastika**. The party insignia was also designed along the same lines: a white disk on a red field, with

the **swastika** in the middle. A Munich goldsmith by the name of Fuss furnished the first usable design, which was kept.

[Chamberlain and Fay's Translation]
In the same sense, arm bands were immediately ordered for the supervising detachments, that is a red band which also shows a white circle with a black **swastika**. The party emblem, too, was designed along the same lines: a white circle in a red field and in its center the **swastika**. A Munch goldsmith, Fuss, produced the first design that could be used and that then was kept.

[Murphy's Translation]
At the same time we immediately ordered the corresponding armlets for our squad of men who kept order at meetings, armlets of red material, a central white disc with the black **swastika** upon it. Herr Fuss, a Munich goldsmith, supplied the first practical and permanent design.

[Dugdale's Translation]
Armlets, also, of the same were at once ordered for the men of the bodies for keeping order—red with a white disc and **hooked cross** in it.

*Als nationale Sozialisten sehen wir in unserer Flagge unser Programm. Im Rot sehen wir den sozialen Gedanken der Bewegung, im Weiß den nationalsozialistischen, im **Hakenkreuz** die Mission des Kampfes für den Sieg des arischen Menschen und zugleich mit ihm auch den Sieg des Gedankens der schaffenden Arbeit, die selbst ewig antisemitisch war und antisemitisch sein wird.*

[Manheim's Translation]
As National Socialists, we see our program in our flag. In red we see the social idea of the movement, in white the nationalistic idea, in the **swastika** the mission of the struggle for the victory of the Aryan man, and, by the same token, the victory of the idea of creative work, which as such always has been and always will be anti-Semitic.

[Chamberlain and Fay's Translation]
As National Socialists we see our program in our flag. In the red we see the social idea of the movement, in the white the national idea, in the **swastika** the mission of the fight for the victory of Aryan man, and at the same time also the victory of the idea of creative work which in itself is and will always be anti-Semitic.

[Murphy's Translation]
We National Socialists regarded our flag as being the embodiment of our party programme. The red expressed the social thought underlying the movement. White the national thought. And the **swastika** signified the mission allotted to us—the struggle for the victory of Aryan mankind and at the same time the triumph of the idea of creative work which is in itself and always will be anti-Semitic.

[In Dugdale's translation this section was omitted and not translated.]

When we compare the original text and various translations, the following is revealed. First, the English word "swastika" is clearly not the word that Hitler used in the original German when he explained the Nazi German emblem. Hitler's word is "Hakenkreuz," as explained previously. The swastika is selected as an English word to refer to the Hakenkreuz in translations by Manheim, Chamberlain and Fay, and Murphy.

Second, although three translations used "swastika" for the Hakenkreuz, the oldest translation by E. Dugdale instead used the literal translation, "hooked cross." Also, Dugdale used "the cross" to refer to the Hakenkreuz. It shows that the Hakenkreuz was considered a type of cross at least in the earlier days of Hitler's reign. This parallels the word choices in the *New York Times*, which in the early 1930s also chose to use the word "Hakenkreuz" rather than "swastika" prior to the publication of the article "Hooked Cross an Old Symbol" referred to earlier.

Thirdly, issues of censorship have long surrounded *Mein Kampf* so that whole texts were not available because of its racist and anti-Semitic content. The Dugdale version is missing two important parts that explain how the Hakenkreuz design was made and what it signified. Omitting this information leaves the reader with an unexplained mystery as to what the symbol meant to Hitler.

[2] Choice of words in Translation

The word "Hakenkreuz" was no doubt a key term when translating *Mein Kampf* and it was necessary for each translator to choose what they believed was the best word or phrase among all possibilities.

Sometimes there is one word or one phrase that is the most difficult and controversial when translating a larger historical experience or concept from how it was originally described in another language. In my tradition of Jodoshinshu Buddhism, there is a Japanese word, Tariki, which is considered key to our understanding of Buddhism. The word literally means "other-power," but the concept it represents is rather complicated and easily misunderstood, and therefore very difficult to translate. How to translate it has been continually discussed and debated in my sect for many decades, and I myself have been involved with some of these translation projects where the question has arisen. Translation is not an easy task, especially when a particular word or phrase carries an important, unique, and complex meaning as the words "Tariki" and "Hakenkreuz" do.

A translator's goal is always to provide a semantic equivalent between the source and target language. In this case, the source language is German and the target language is English. There is no such thing as a perfect translation and the choice for what word to use may be different depending upon each translator. There are many things that can affect these choices, such as cultural bias, depth of understanding of the text, etc.

How did translators of *Mein Kampf* choose their word for "Hakenkreuz" among several possible choices? The first choice is to not translate and just use the German word "Hakenkreuz" that Hitler used. This is called "borrowing." Borrowing happens often when equivalent words do not exist in the target language. For example, the Japanese word "sushi" is not translated into English but is instead borrowed from the Japanese language. Another example is the title of *Mein Kampf.* When translating the title, the 1943, 1940, and 1939 translations borrowed directly from the German title *Mein Kampf* without translation. The 1933 Dugdale version, in contrast, translated the title literally as "My Struggle" in the British publication, and as "My Battle" in the American one. None of the translators of *Mein Kampf* used the borrowed word "Hakenkreuz," although it is definitely one possible choice.

The second choice is to translate the meaning of "Hakenkreuz" as Hook-Cross, or hooked cross, because the word consists of "Haken" which means "hook, curve, bend" in German, and "kreuz" which means "cross." This is the choice made in the 1933 Dugdale translation, where he semantically and literally translated "Hakenkreuz" as "hooked cross." Dugdale treated the word "Hakenkreuz" as a regular phrase/noun, but Hitler used the word to represent a symbol that had a particular meaning and shape meant for the specific use as an emblem for his party. This word was a proper noun, and therefore the term "Hook-Cross" should be used as the most accurate translation to for the unique Nazi symbol. To not write it as a proper noun can possibly convey the more general meaning of the Eastern swastika, and is therefore a mistranslation.

When German people heard the word "Hakenkreuz," they could immediately understand the symbol as a type of cross. Translating Hitler's symbol as "Hook-Cross," clearly and properly conveys that Hitler's symbol was not being used as a version of a swastika, a word which Hitler himself significantly and deliberately chose not to use, but instead as a version of a cross.

The third choice is to use one of the existing words already used in English to refer to the symbol's form or shape. Such words included: swastika, gammadion, Croix gammee, fylfot, and whirling log. The name "swastika" gained popularity among these terms in the West at the end of 19th century.[274] Therefore it is understandable that some translators choose the term "swastika" instead of the other words listed above. According to the OED, the term "swastika" was first used in English in 1871,[275] and was first used in English to refer to the Nazi emblem in 1932.[276] This was the choice made for the *Mein Kampf* translations of Manheim, Chamberlain and Fay, and Murphy.

But "swastika" was not truly a proper and accurate translation because it did not translate the *meaning* of the word "Hakenkreuz," but rather was simply an attempt to describe the *shape* of the Nazi insignia. Three *Mein Kampf* translations chose to use the word "swastika," which is a variation of a borrowed Sanskrit word "svastika."

The swastika was already known at the time as a word that could express the shape of the Hakenkreuz. It was also known to represent a "lucky" sign from the East, and was a word and symbol already linked to the word "Aryan" through Muller's Aryan Language Theory. It could thus convey the newly popularized notion of an Aryan race that Hitler further related to anti-Semitism based upon his concept of the imagined pure blood of Aryans. In this sense the word "swastika" was able to convey many elements of the meaning of the Hakenkreuz as well as its shape, although it was not truly accurate.

The word "swastika" may have been somewhat inaccurate from the perspective of the art of translation, but more significantly, the biggest problem with that choice is that it ended up completely erasing the word

"Hakenkreuz" in English, thus altering the definition of the word "swastika" in English and in turn altering the perceived meaning of the symbol. The meaning of Hitler's Hakenkreuz symbol obliterated the meaning of the Eastern swastika in popular perception. Many people now believe that not just the symbol but also the *word* "swastika" was created by Hitler. The mistranslation and its ongoing usage have created the illusion that the swastika *is* Hitler, and it has changed the meaning to that of all that is evil, the complete reversal of its original meaning. There is no doubt that the word "swastika" was damaged by these translations. The Hakenkreuz has invaded and poisoned the swastika and has denied any other definition and signification of all other swastikas and other uses other than the meaning of what should be properly termed a Hakenkreuz or hook-cross in English.

In comparison to other languages, using the word "swastika" in English as an equivalent for the Hakenkreuz, although it made sense in some ways, was still a bit of a leap. When *Mein Kampf* was translated into European languages other than English, translators tended to use more literal translations. Many dictionaries in other languages have two entries to make the distinction between "swastika" and "Hakenkreuz". From this perspective, speculations of intentional usage of "swastika" instead of "Hakenkreuz" by the British and American translators to protect the cross are not necessarily out of order. Except for the first translation by Dugdale, English translations were done during World War II (1939–1945). These translations might include an invisible agenda rather than a simple translation. The Dugdale translation of "Hakenkreuz" as "hooked cross" makes sense then, when compared to the other three translations during the war. We know that many things made during wartime tend to have a hidden agenda existing beyond their surface agenda. It is therefore very reasonable to doubt the use of the word "swastika" was simply a random translation choice and was possibly part of wartime propaganda.

Just as a coin has a front side and back side, the translations have two sides. From the Eastern religious point of view, the translators, though perhaps unintentionally, helped mistreat, desecrate, and disrespect the sacred symbol of the swastika. Eastern religions were desecrated in many ways from this.

On the other hand, the Christian cross was saved from similar desecration through association with Hitler's actions. The accusation that the Hakenkreuz is an anti-Semitic symbol did not desecrate all crosses.

Though racial discrimination and anti-Semitism were carried out under Hitler's Cross, English speakers do not see the cross in the swastika. These evil actions were instead done under Hitler's Swastika. If we call it a Hook-Cross, people may be more likely to recognize the cross in the center of the swastika-cross. Whether intentional or not, these translators protected the Christian cross and damaged the Eastern religious swastika. Intentionally or not, these translators succeeded in protecting the cross. The word "swastika" hid the cross very well. Hitler's Nazi Germany murdered millions of people under a cross (crusade), but many in the West think that Hitler murdered under the swastika. The swastika, in effect, has saved the cross from association with Hitler in the English-speaking world. But in doing so, the swastika also became a scapegoat for Hitler's actions.

Present and Future Meaning of the Swastika Symbol

Abraham Joshua Heschel (1907–1972), who is considered one of the most influential Jewish theologians of the 20th century, wrote in *The Prophets,*

> What impairs our sight are habits of seeing as well as the mental concomitants of seeing. Our sight is suffused with knowing, instead of feeling painfully the lack of knowing what we see. The principle to be kept in mind is to know what we see rather than to see what we know.[277]

The principle of "to know what we see rather than to see what we know" is a very challenging thing in our lives. We all experience to some degree times when our preconceived knowledge stops us from moving forward. In my Buddhist tradition, we also emphasize seeing things as they are, not simply as we want to see. Only from such a foundation can we move forward.

Current Swastika Issues

[1] Hindu-Jewish Leadership Summit in 2008

During the Second Hindu-Jewish Leadership Summit, held in Jerusalem in 2008, a joint declaration recognizing the larger history of the swastika was made. Its item #7 said:

> Svastika is an ancient and greatly auspicious symbol of the Hindu tradition. It is inscribed on Hindu temples, ritual

altars, entrances, and even account books. A distorted version of this sacred symbol was misappropriated by the Third Reich in Germany, and abused as an emblem under which heinous crimes were perpetrated against humanity, particularly the Jewish people. The participants recognize that this symbol is, and has been sacred to Hindus for millennia, long before its misappropriation.[278]

As religious leaders have already recognized the swastika, in my view as a Buddhist, we need to now implement this declaration by developing educational materials and workshops to inform the English-speaking public of its larger history and usage. This is already starting to occur.

[2] ADL's Historic Announcement

On July 27, 2010, the Anti-Defamation League (ADL) made a historic announcement about the swastika symbol. the *Jewish Week* reported,

> The painting of a swastika—the dark, ubiquitous signature of hateful vandals everywhere—will no longer be automatically considered an act of anti-Semitism under new guidelines for recording attacks against Jews announced by the Anti-Defamation League. The most prominent Jewish defense agency in the country, perhaps the world, announced July 27 that it has revamped its guidelines for recording anti-Semitic incidents in its annual survey for the first time in 30 years, taking a more conservative approach.[279]

In a recent article dated November 11, 2011, the *Jewish Week* reported, "The ADL recently announced that it no longer considers the swastika an outright anti-Semitic symbol for purposes of recording hate crimes statistics if the target is not related to Jews."[280]

The swastika has in recent years become more of a general hate symbol rather than one which is particularly anti-Semitic. This can be seen in a number of recent incidents in New York. On January 11, 2012, DNAinfo News reported the following:[281]

> MIDTOWN—Vandals accused of scrawling swastikas on storefronts near Bryant Park were captured on security video footage. The NYPD released film of four people wanted for the attacks on the Penguin Clothing Store, the Kinokuniya

Bookstore and an office building, all on one block of Sixth Avenue. It shows two females and two males leaving the bookstore on Sunday. It shows one of them stopping to draw a swastika. One of the male suspects was shown pulling a black wheelbag and carrying a red backpack, police said.

Kinokuniya is a Japanese bookstore, and has nothing to do with Jewish people or Judaism. Why did they paint a swastika at a Japanese store? What exactly were they trying to communicate? It was not clear. There was no hate message that accompanied the symbol, and the suspects were not apprehended so there has been no chance to ask them.

[3] Disturbing News

An especially dramatic incident of apparent anti-Semitism happened on the 73rd Anniversary of *Kristallnacht* on November 11, 2011. The *New York Times* reported the story under the headline, "Cars Burned and Swastikas Scrawled in Brooklyn Jewish Area":

> One or more vandals on Friday set fire to several parked cars and scrawled anti-Semitic graffiti on nearby benches in Brooklyn, in what the police said was a hate crime in a heavily Jewish neighborhood. The arson took place along Ocean Parkway in Midwood, between Avenue I and Avenue J, where three cars, a BMW, a Lexus and a Jaguar, were set on fire. Also, "KKK" was written on the side of a red van, the police said, and swastikas and anti-Semitic slurs were scrawled on benches.[282]

"This kind of hateful act has no place in the freest city in the freest country in the world," said Mayor Michael Bloomberg. His remarks were echoed by other local leaders. Two days later residents, elected officials and activists marched against hate and intolerance.

But, the story did not end. Two months later after an investigation, police announced they suspected that the incident was an insurance scam, and not a hate crime, with the hateful graffiti done to throw off investigators. NBC reporter Shimon Prokupecz, in a report written on January 11, 2012, said, "Authorities are investigating a spree of burned cars and swastikas in a predominantly Jewish area of Brooklyn as a possible insurance scam, not a hate crime, sources tell NBC New York." The same report explained,

> Officials have a person of interest that they're investigating for being behind the November destruction, which included spray-painted "KKK" graffiti and stunned the city with its hateful messages. The person may have been trying to destroy a car for insurance money, authorities believe, and was concealing that with the other crimes.[283]

It is reasonable to say that those who committed these ill actions with ill intentions used the swastika for a hateful and destructive purpose, no matter what their own backgrounds were. But what about the jewelry store mentioned in the opening chapter of this book? The shop carried items with swastika symbols and identified them as Tibetan symbols of good luck, not a hate symbol. Should this symbol be removed and the person selling it described as evil?

The passion with which the earrings were criticized was similar to the reaction to hate crimes. The very appearance of the symbol was enough to draw ire, even well outside of the context of a hate crime, even when it was explained by the manager and publicized in news reports that the earrings were not meant to be Nazi swastikas. Selling an ancient Eastern religious symbol represented as such is not a hate crime. The reaction to this incident shows that it is time to talk about the swastika symbol more openly. These types of incidents will happen more often when the East and West meet.

Assemblyman Dov Hikind, whose constituents that he is elected to represent include many Asian Americans, after being informed of the Asian manager's explanation of it as an ancient Tibetan symbol said: "The average person, when they see a swastika, they see it as a symbol of hate. End of story." In the news story, the manager was correct in describing the symbol as meaning good fortune in Tibetan Buddhism. On the other hand, Hikind's statement also was correct by saying that the swastika is equated with evil in the West. Now, when this conflict happens, what should we do? This is where interreligious dialogue and mutual understanding become important. When one side is happy, the other side is unhappy, and vice versa. In the news, there was no dialogue, just opposing voices isolated from one another, and usually as in this case, the louder and stronger voice wins.

Where Are We Going?

The most important aspect of dialogue is to be able to listen to others, and understand the other's position as well as presenting one's own view. Dialogue cannot be achieved if one is not ready to listen to others. Religious dialogue, interfaith dialogue, and intercultural dialogue are the way to work together to find a common ground with mutual respect and mutual understanding. When it comes to the swastika symbol, we need to begin by providing information and knowledge first.

When I traveled to Europe to visit concentration camps in Auschwitz, Treblinka, and Sachsenhausen, and the Anne Frank Museum, I did so because I felt that as a Buddhist priest, this was important for me to do as I embarked on my journey toward understanding both the light and dark of the swastika symbol. I needed to personally stand on the very ground where millions of people—men, woman, children, adults and elderly—lost their lives, to first offer prayer and meditation and light incense in respect to these precious lives.

I also met with the Chief Rabbi of Poland, Michael Schudrich, of the Nozyk Synagogue in the Warsaw Ghetto, the only pre-war synagogue still active in Warsaw today. When I mentioned about the swastika being considered as a "universal symbol of evil" in the US, Schudrich immediately said, "It's not." It wasn't surprising that Rabbi Schudrich would know about its origins because he served as a rabbi in Japan for six years and must have seen the manji-swastika there. He added, "However, 99% of the time when somebody draws a swastika on walls in Europe, it is something negative. People who write the symbol have no idea that the symbol comes from Buddhism or Hinduism." Rabbi Schudrich pointed out that the swastika is "such a powerful symbol of evil." It is not logical, intellectual, or political, but rather it is "emotional" coming from the historical fact that millions of Jews were killed under the swastika symbol, he explained.

Rabbi Schudrich suggested that I create a statement about the Eastern meaning of the swastika symbol that could be displayed at Holocaust-related sites and museums, as well as statements about its meaning in the West that could be placed at Eastern sites where it appears, such as the Senso-ji temple in Asakusa.

We all need to have knowledge, and to educate ourselves from broader perspectives, based upon facts and truth. We may not like some facts and truth, but yet we need to learn from them. Our lives are full of learning. It is always good to be humble and open-minded. Seeing the swastika symbol as an interfaith issue has been eye opening for me. Before I came to this country, it was just a simple Buddhist symbol that I grew up with in Japan. This does not mean that I did not learn about the Holocaust. Students in Japan learn about it in school. But the Nazi symbol is taught to us as a separate symbol with a separate word, "Hakenkreuz," used to describe it. Although it clearly looks similar to a manji in design, there are visual differences as well: the Hakenkreuz is right turning and it is tilted while the manji is usually left turning, and untilted. The Hakenkreuz always appears with the red and white background. Therefore it is easy for Japanese to see the two symbols as distinct. The nature of the Japanese language compared to English and other Western languages is also significant to understand why it is easy for Japanese to readily comprehend these two symbols as distinct. Japanese makes use of Chinese characters, or "kanji" as they are called, in its written language. These characters consist of symbols to represent words that may be homonyms yet have a distinct meaning. Often these kanji look similar to other kanji, yet have subtle differences, often of a single stroke, imparting a different meaning. Therefore, in the Japanese understanding of the meaning of a particular visual symbol, differences that may seem small or be overlooked entirely in Western eyes may be magnified to a Japanese who is already used to that as part of our everyday language system.

I was shocked to hear from a hate-crime expert that "swastika is now the universal symbol of hate or Nazism." However, I never would have learned that the swastika was such a universal symbol, represented in many religious traditions, if I had not embarked on this research. I hope that this work will provide a new awareness about the wider meaning of the swastika symbol, and offer new ways of approaching the international, historical, and religiously diverse swastika symbol, as well as an understanding of how Hitler adopted the Hook-Cross from the Eastern swastika. In order to prevent something like the Holocaust from happening again, we must understand as much as we can about how it occurred. Buddhism emphasizes the importance of awareness. Hitler's usage of the symbol was an important part of that process, and understanding how and why he chose it is vital to insure nothing like that ever happens again to humanity. It is a lesson in how important symbols are, whether they are used for religious, political, or any other purpose, light or dark.

Buddhism is about change. I hope to see the symbol of the swastika transformed in the West. In Buddhism, another symbol is also frequently used, that of the lotus flower, which grows out of the mud, representing enlightenment. I hope to see the swastika grow out of the dark muddy swamp of history through recognition of the swastika of the East and other world cultures, and by promoting discussion and dialogue in relation to the swastika and the Hook-Cross in the West.

In Buddhism, "transformation" means "change" or "turning" specifically by providing and receiving knowledge and understanding. Transformation in this case does *not* mean to forget the swastika's desecration by the Nazis or trying to replace that historical usage, but rather to remember it and to face the symbol's entire history directly. False and incorrect information causes confusion and chaos, but true and correct knowledge creates understanding and balance. The current situation in the West presents a very one-sided and unbalanced view of what the swastika symbol represents. As noted in the opening chapter, the lotus flower is a Buddhist symbol of enlightenment achieved through transformation. The lotus flower only blossoms from the mud, not from ordinary beautiful soil. The symbol exists to remind us that suffering is a source of enlightenment, and without suffering, there will be no enlightenment. In the midst of suffering and pain, the beautiful lotus thrives and emerges. This teaches us that through right knowledge and wisdom with compassion, the pure flower that is ourselves will be healed and nurtured.

Discussion, debate, and dialogue about the swastika can help create transformation not just of the swastika. It can also provide opportunities to talk about larger and related issues of hate crimes, religious symbols, freedom of religious expression, the meaning and power of symbols, and genocide and how the Holocaust occurred.

Once we gain knowledge about the swastika, we no longer need to fear the symbol as it exists in its original contexts, and can accept its dark history and bring light to darkness. Because anti-Semitism has deeply hurt human society, it is not so easy to change overnight the image of the swastika symbol as distinct from the Hook-Cross. It is likewise also important for Eastern people to understand the pain of the Holocaust and what Hitler's version of the symbol means within that context.

Action Plan for the Public

If you believe that you can damage, then believe that you can fix.
If you believe that you can harm, then believe that you can heal.[284]

I hope to eventually create a statement that could be provided to Holocaust sites as well as Eastern religious sites about the comprehensive history of the swastika as Rabbi Schudrich suggested. This could be a way to educate people about the larger history of the swastika and its ongoing usage in other cultures. As millions of people from all over the world visit museums such as the Auschwitz Holocaust Memorial Museum, as well as major temples in Asia such as Senso-ji in Tokyo, it is a practical and efficient approach to educate people about this subject.

During visits I have made to Holocaust museums as well as Holocaust sites in Europe such as Auschwitz, I was struck by the fact that there are no explanations displayed about the differences between Hitler's Hook-Cross (Hakenkreuz) and the Eastern swastika. As a Buddhist priest, when I made these visits, I felt heavy, dark, and sad about what happened to the Jews, Gypsies, prisoners of war, handicapped, homosexual, and all victims. But at the same time, I felt uncomfortable that there was no explanation of the swastika beyond Hitler's usage. The sacred swastika continues its defilement without any proper explanation. Likewise, it would be helpful to have written explanations at Japanese temples where the swastika is used prominently, such as Senso-ji and Zenko-ji, to help visitors understand what the symbol means. While visiting both during a trip to Japan in 2010, I observed many confused tourists wondering about their presence.

Here are sample suggestions:

Suggested Statement about the Swastika for Western Museums

The swastika symbol, or "svastika" as it is called in Sanskrit, is said by scholars to be one of the oldest sacred symbols in the world. Its use has been documented in early Christianity, Judaism, and many Eastern religions as well as Native American Indian cultures. Scholars believe its original meaning may have been to represent the sun.

The swastika has been used for more than 2,000 years in Buddhism, Hinduism, and Jainism as a sacred religious symbol of auspiciousness, luck, and virtue. It is seen in temples, scrolls, statues, and other ritual items used in these religions.

In many Asian cultures, the swastika is also commonly used as a decorative element in ceramics, textiles, woodwork and other items as a lucky motif.

Hitler, who had an interest in Eastern religions and the occult, misappropriated and misinterpreted the swastika symbol, which he called a "Hook-Cross," or "Hakenkreuz" in German, for use in political propaganda. Likewise Hitler also misappropriated the Sanskrit word "Aryan," whose original meaning simply meant "noble" and "virtuous" in Buddhism and other Indian religions without any connotation of race or ethnicity. Taken out of their original meanings and contexts, the swastika and concept of "Aryan" served the Nazi propaganda helping to create the tragedy of World War II and the Holocaust.

Hitler's use of the swastika was a desecration of the symbol. Since then, it has been commonly associated in the West with anti-Semitism, Hitler, Neo-Nazi supremacy groups, racism, and hate crimes, in contrast to its continued positive associations in the East.

Suggested Statement about the Swastika for Eastern Tradition Temples

Visitors may notice many swastika symbols at this temple. It is not here as a symbol of Nazi Germany or hate groups, as it is commonly associated with in the West.

The swastika symbol, or "svastika" as it is called in Sanskrit, is said by scholars to be one of the oldest sacred symbols in the world. Its use has been documented in early Christianity, Judaism, and many Eastern religions as well as Native American Indian cultures. Scholars believe its original meaning may have been to represent the sun.

The swastika has been used for more than 2,000 years in Buddhism, Hinduism, and Jainism as a sacred religious symbol of auspiciousness, luck, and virtue. It is seen in temples, scrolls, statues, and other ritual items used in these religions.

In many Asian cultures, the swastika is also commonly used as a decorative element in ceramics, textiles, woodwork, and other items as a lucky motif.

Hitler, who had an interest in Eastern religions and the occult, misappropriated and misinterpreted the swastika symbol, which he called a "Hook-Cross," or "Hakenkreuz" in German, for use in political propaganda. Likewise Hitler also misappropriated the Sanskrit word "Aryan," whose original meaning simply meant "noble" and "virtuous" in Buddhism and other Indian religions without any connotation of race or ethnicity. Taken out of their original meanings and contexts, the swastika and concept of "Aryan" served the Nazi propaganda helping to create the tragedy of World War II and the Holocaust.

Hitler's use of the swastika was a desecration of the symbol. Since then, it has been commonly associated in the West with anti-Semitism, Hitler, Neo-Nazi supremacy groups, racism, and hate crimes, in contrast to its continued positive associations in the East.

* * *

Talking about the swastika symbol is a way to create more dialogue about both issues of genocide and an understanding of diverse religious communities. Mutual understanding and respect is at the heart of all interfaith work. As we educate the West about the swastika, we also have a chance to educate the East about the horrors of the Holocaust, which often is not discussed in depth in Eastern countries such as Japan. In this sense, the swastika, through discussions about its use and meanings, can create a two-way path in the 21st century, reminding us of "Never Again" and helping to prevent future genocide in the world. In this way, this original sun symbol, a symbol possibly as old as human history itself, can shine a light of education and mutual understanding. When seen in this way, the swastika's cross shape itself inspires, consisting of two lines together symbolizing a meeting of East and West, in unity and harmony.

The meanings of Aryan and Swastika are written In Japanese as
聖 (Aryan) and 万徳 (swastika). If you combine these two words, it creates the compound 聖徳 (Aryan Swastika), which is read in Japanese as
"Shotoku." This is the name of Prince Shotoku, who brought Buddhism
to Japan and created the first constitution of Japan in 604, The Seven-
teen Chapters constitution. It was based upon the Buddhist principles of
peace and harmony. One of my favorite chapters, Chapter 10, talks about
"ordinary people." It says:

> Let us control ourselves and not be resentful when others
> disagree with us, for all men have hearts and each heart has
> its own leanings. The right of others is our wrong, and our
> right is their wrong. We are not unquestionably sages, nor
> are they unquestionably fools. Both of us are simply ordinary
> men. How can anyone lay down a rule by which to distinguish
> right from wrong? For we are all wise sometimes and foolish
> at others. Therefore, though others give way to anger, let us on
> the contrary dread our own faults ...[285]

For me personally, protecting the "swastika" and "Arya" means protecting the most important figure of Japanese Buddhism, Prince Shotoku.
Buddhism in Japan began with the Aryan-Swastika (聖徳) Prince, and I
am one of the recipients of rich and profound teachings of Buddhism
and Prince Shotoku. This is also a new finding for me but this discovery
encouraged me to continue my project and bring a real "Aryan" way of
life to our society. All of us can be an Aryan, regardless of race, ethnicity,
sexual orientation, and age, just by practicing the "noble" truths and lib-
erating ourselves from delusions created by greed, anger, and ignorance.
By so doing, we will live up to the symbol of the swastika, which is light,
life, liberty, and luck, shining on all beings like the sun. The Aryan swastika in Buddhism is the way of peace, non-violence, and happiness to all
with wisdom and compassion. From a Buddhist perspective, the Aryan
Swastika represents the path to overcome sufferings and sorrows from
the dark shadow of the history of human race. May the sacred sun rise
again for real peace and harmony to all humanity.

Bibliography

Books

Aachen, Albert of. Edited and translated by Susan B. Edgington. *Albert of Aachen: Historia Ierosolimitana, History of the Journey to Jerusalem.* New York: Oxford University Press, 2007.

Abe, Masao and Heine, Steven. *Buddhism and Interfaith Dialogue: Part One of a Two-Volume Sequel to Zen and Western Thought.* Hawaii: University of Hawaii Press, 1995.

Aigner, Dennis J. *The Swastika Symbol in Navajo Textiles.* Laguna Beach, CA: DAI Press 2000.

Anderson, Ken. *Hitler and the Occult.* New York: Prometheus Books, 1995.

App, Urs. *Richard Wagner and Buddhism.* Rorschach, Switzerland: UniversityMedia, 2011.

Arendt, Hannah. *The Origins of Totalitarianism.* New York: Harcourt, Brace & World, 1966.

Awasaka, Tsumao. *Manji no Maryoku, Tomoe no Juryoku (Mystical Power of Manji and Tomoe).* Tokyo: Shinchosha, 2008.

Bassed, Peter. *Wagner's Parsifal: The Journey of a Soul.* Cambridge, MA: Wakefield Press. 2000.

Berling, Judith A. *Understanding Other Religious Worlds: A Guide for Interreligious Education.* Maryknoll, NY: Orbis Books, 2004.

Bergen, Doris. *Twisted Cross: The German Christian Movement in the Third Reich.* Chapel Hill, NC: University of North Carolina Press, 1996.

_____. *War & Genocide: A Concise History of the Holocaust.* Lanham, MD: Rowman & Littlefield, 2003.

Bernstein, Alison R. *American Indians and World War II: Toward a New Era in Indian Affairs.* Norman, OK: University of Oklahoma Press, 1999.

Bhalla, Prem P. *Hindu Rites, Rituals, Customs and Traditions.* Delhi, India: Pustak Mahal, 2006.

Bonvillain, Nancy. *Language, Culture, and Communication: The Meaning of Messages.* Upper Saddle River, NJ: Pearson Prentice Hall, 2008.

Brener, Milton. *Richard Wagner And the Jews.* Jefferson, NC: McFarland, 2005.

Brown, William Norman. *The Swastika: A Study of the Nazi Claims of its Aryan Origin.* New York: Emerson Books, Inc., 1933.

Browning, Christopher R. *The Origins of the Final Solution: The Evolution of Nazi Jewish Policy, September 1939-March 1942.* Lincoln, NE: University of Nebraska Press, 2004.

Bryant, Edwin Francis. *The Indo-Aryan Controversy: Evidence and Inference in Indian History.* New York: Routledge, 2005.

Budge, Wallis E.A. *Amulets and Superstitions (1930).* Whitefish, MT: Kessinger Publishing, 2003.

Buko, Andrzej. *The Archaeology of Early Medieval Poland: Discoveries—Hypotheses—Interpretations.* Boston, MA: Brill, 2008.

Burton, Dan and Grandy, David. *Magic, Mystery, and Science: The Occult in Western Civilization.* Bloomington, IN: Indiana University Press, 2004.

Campbell, Joseph. *The Flight of the Wild Gander; Explorations in the Mythological Dimension.* New York: Viking Press, 1969.

Carroll, James. *Constantine's Sword: The Church and the Jews: A History.* Boston, MA: Houghton Mifflin, 2001.

Chalk, Frank and Jonassohn, Kurt. *The History and Sociology of Genocide: Analyses and Case Studies.* New Haven, CT: Yale UP, 1990.

Chamberlain, Houston S. *Foundation of the Nineteenth Century: With an Introduction by Lord Redesdale. (Volume 1 and Volume 2).* Munchen, Germany: F. Bruckmann, 1911.

_____. Translated by Ainslie Hight. *Richard Wagner.* London: J.M. Dent, 1900.

Clube, Victor and Napier, Bill. *The Cosmic Serpent: A Catastrophist View of Earth History.* New York: Universe Books, 1982.

Conway, David. *Jewry in Music: Entry to the Profession from the Enlightenment to Richard Wagner.* Cambridge: Cambridge University Press 2011.

Conway, John S. *The Nazi Persecution of the Churches, 1933–1945.* New York: Basic Books, 1968.

Cort, John E. *Jains in the World: Religious Values and Ideology in India.* Oxford: Oxford University Press, 2001.

Crowley, Terry and Bowern, Claire. *An Introduction to Historical Linguistics.* New York: Oxford University Press Inc., 2010.

Davidson, H.R. Ellis. *Gods and Myths of Northern Europe.* Baltimore, MD: Penguin Books, 1964.

Dawidowicz, Lucy. *The War Against the Jews 1933–1945.* New York: Bantam, 1986.

Dillistone, F. W. *The Power of Symbols in Religion and Culture.* London: SCM Press, 1986.

Dreisbach, Donald F. *Symbols & Salvation: Paul Tillich's Doctrine of Religious Symbols and his Interpretation of the Symbols of the Christian Tradition.* Lanham, MD: University Press of America, 1993.

Eck, Diana L. *Banaras: City of Light.* New York: Columbia University Press, 1999.

Engelmann, Bernt. *In Hitler's Germany: Everyday Life in the Third Reich*. New York: Pantheon Books, 1986.

Enthoven, R.E. *The Folklore of Bombay*. London: The Clarendon Press, 1924.

Falk, Avner. *Anti-Semitism: A History and Psychoanalysis of Contemporary Hatred*. Westport, CT: Praeger Publishers, 2008.

Fest, Joachim C. Translated by Richard and Clara Winston. *Hitler*. New York: Harcourt Brace Jovanovich, 1974.

Feuerstein, Georg and Kak, Subhash. *The Search of the Cradle of Civilization: New Light on Ancient India*. New Deli: Motilal Banarsidass Publisher, 2008.

Fiset, Louis and Nomura, Gail M. *Nikkei in the Pacific Northwest: Japanese American and Japanese Canadian in the Twentieth Century*. Seattle, WA: The University of Washington Press, 2005.

Flood, Charles Bracelen. *Hitler: The Path to Power*. Boston, MA: Houghton Mifflin Company, 1989.

Fuchs, Thomas. *A Concise Biography of Adolf Hitler*. New York: Berkley Books, 1990.

Gere, Cathy. *The Tomb of Agamemnon*. Cambridge, MA: Harvard University Press, 2006.

Gobineau, Arthur de. Translated by Adrian Collins. *The Inequality of Human Race*. London: William Heinmmann, 1915.

Goblet d'Alviella, Eugene. *The Migration of Symbols*. Westminster, UK: Archibald Constable and Co., 1894.

Goldhagen, Daniel Jonah. *Hitler's Willing Executioners*. New York: Vintage, 1997.

Goldsmith, Elizabeth. *Life Symbols as Related to Sex Symbolism* (originally published in 1923). Whitefish, MT: Kessinger Publishing, 2003.

Goodrick-Clarke, Nicholas. *Hitler's priestess: Savitri Devi, the Hindu-Aryan myth, and neo-Nazism*. New York: New York University Press, 1998.

_____. *The Occult Roots of Nazism: The Ariosophists of Austria and Germany, 1890–1935*. Wellingborough, Northamptonshire, UK: Aquarian Press, 1985.

Goodyear, William H. *The Grammar of the Lotus: A New History of Classic Ornament as a Development of Sun Worship*. London: Sampson Low, Marston & Co, 1891.

Greg, Robert Philips. *On the Meaning and Origin of the Fylfot and Swastika*. Westminster, UK: Nichols and Sons, 1884.

Gritsch, Eric W. *Martin Luther's Anti-Semitism: Against His Better Judgment*. Grand Rapids, MI: Wm. B. Eerdmans Publishing Co., 2012.

Gunji, Takeshi. *Bukkyo Shin Hakken (Buddhism New Discovery): Zenko-ji, September Issue*. Tokyo: Asahishinbun-sha, 2007.

Gutmann, Joseph. *Iconography of Religions: Judaism. The Jewish Sanctuary*. Leiden, Netherlands: BRILL, 1983.

Hale, Christopher. *Himmler's Crusade: The Nazis' expedition to find the origins of the Aryan Race*. Hoboken, NJ: John Wiley & Sons, 2003.

Harley, J. B. and Woodward, David. *The History of Cartography: Cartography in the Traditional Islamic and South Asian Societies.* Chicago, IL: The University of Chicago Press, 1992.

Hanh, Thich Nhat. *The Heart of the Buddha's Teaching: Transforming Suffering into Peace, Joy and Liberation.* Berkeley, CA: Parallax Press, 1998.

Heidegger, Martin. Translated by Peter D. Hertz. *On the Way to Language.* San Francisco: Harper & Row, 1971.

Heiden, Konrad. *Der Fuehrer: Hitler's Rise to Power.* Boston, MA: Beacon Press, 1969.

Heidenrich, Alfred. The Catacombs: *Pictures from the Life of Early Christianity, 2nd Edition.* London: The Christian Community Press, 1962.

Heller, Steven. *The Swastika: Symbol Beyond Redemption?* New York: Allworth Press, 2000.

Henderson, William James. *Richard Wagner: His Life and His Dramas.* New York: G. P. Putnam's sons, 1923.

Heschel, Abraham Joshua. *The Prophets.* New York: HarperCollins, 2001.

Heschel, Susannah. *The Aryan Jesus: Christian Theologians and the Bible in Nazi Germany.* Princeton, NJ: Princeton University Press, 2008.

Hitler, Adolf. *Mein Kampf.* München, Germany: Zentralverlag der NSDAP, Frz. Eher Nachf., 1940.

_____. Editorial Sponsors: John Chamberlain and Sidney Fay and others. *Mein Kampf, Complete and Unabridged.* New York: Reynal & Hitchcock, 1940.

_____. Translated by Ralph Manheim. *Mein Kampf.* Boston: Houghton Mifflin, 1943.

_____. Translated and annotated by James Murphy. *Mein Kampf.* London: Hutchison & Co., 1939.

_____. Translated by Eher Nachf. *Mein Kampf.* Elite Minds Inc., 2009.

_____. Translated by E.T.S. Dugdale. *My Battle:* Boston. MA: Houghton Mufflin, 1933.

_____. *Sämtliche Aufzeichnungen: 1905–1924.* Stuttgart, Deutsche: Verlags-Anstalt, 1980.

_____. Edited by Norman H. Baynes. *The Speeches of Adolf Hitler, April 1922-August 1939, Vol. 1.* Oxford: Oxford University Press, 1942.

Howard, John. *Concentration Camps on the Home Front: Japanese Americans in the House of Jim Crow.* Chicago, IL: The University of Chicago Press. 2008.

Inaba, Lawson Fusao. *The Japanese American Internment Experience.* Berkeley, CA: Heyday Books, 2000.

Kashima, Tesuden. *Buddhism in America: The Social Organization of an Ethnic Religions Institution.* Westport, CT: Greenwood Press, 1977.

Kenrick, Donald and Grattan, Puxon. *Gypsies Under the Swastika.* Hatfield, England: University of Hertfordshire Press, 2009.

Kershaw, Ian. *Hitler 1889–1936: Hubris.* New York: W.W. Norton & Company, 1998.

Kertzer, David I. *Ritual, Politics, and Power.* New Haven: Yale University Press, 1988.

Kirkpatrick, Sidney D. *Hitler's Holy Relics: A True Story of Nazi Plunder and the Race to Recover the Crown Jewels of the Holy Roman Empire.* New York: Simon & Schuster, 2010.

Knapp, Stephen. *Avatars, Gods and Goddesses of Vedic Culture: Understanding the Characteristics, Powers and Positions of the Hindu Divinities.* USA: CreateSpace, 2010.

_____. *Proof of Vedic Culture's Global Existence.* USA: Booksurge, 2009.

Kogon, Eugen. *The Theory and Practice of Hell.* New York: Berkley Books, 1998.

Kubizek, August. *The Young Hitler I Knew.* London: Greenhill Books, 2006.

Lal, Braj Basi. *India 1947–1997: New Light on the Indus Civilization.* New Delhi: Aryan Books International, 1998.

Levi, Erik. *Mozart and the Nazis.* New Haven, CT: Yale University Press, 2011.

Lewy, Guenther. *The Catholic Church and Nazi Germany.* New York: McGraw-Hill Book Company, 1964.

List, Guido von. *Das Geheimnis der Runen.* Leipzig, Germany: E. F. Steinacker, 1908.

_____. Translated by Stephen Flowers. *The Secret of the Runes.* Rochester, VT: Inner Traditions, 1988.

Luczanits, Christian. *The Buddhist Heritage of Pakistan: Art of Gandhara [Asia Society Museum, New York, March 1–May 31, 2011].* New York: Asia Society, 2011.

Luther, Martin. Translated by Martin Bertram. *On the Jews and Their Lies, 1543 (Luther's Works Volume 47).* Minneapolis, MN: Fortress Press, 1971.

_____. *The Jews and Their Lies.* Reedy, WV: Liberty Bell Publications, 2004.

_____. Selected by Teodore G. Tappert. *Selected Writings of Martin Luther, Volume 1.* Minneapolis, MN: Fortress Press, 2007.

Lutzer, Erwin W. *Hitler's Cross.* Chicago: Moody Press, 1995.

Lyell, Charles. *Geological Evidences of the Antiquity of Man.* London: Murray, 1863.

MacCulloch, C.J.A. Canon, John A. (Ed.) *Mythology of All Races, vol. 8.* Boston, MA: Marshall Jones Co., 1928.

Magee, Bryan. *Aspects of Wagner, Second Edition, Revised and Enlarged.* Oxford: Oxford University Press; 2nd edition, 1988.

_____. *The Tristan Chord: Wagner and Philosophy.* New York: Henry Holt and Co., 2000.

MacKenzie, Donald A. *Migration of Symbols.* Whitefish, MT: Kessinger Publishing, 2003.

ManWoman. *Gentle Swastika: Reclaiming the Innocence.* Cranbrook, B.C., Canada: Flyfoot Press, 2001.

Marrus, Michael R (Ed.). *The Nazi Holocaust–Part 2: The Origins of the Holocaust.* Westport, CT: Meckler Corporation, 1989.

Maser, Werner. *Hitler's Mein Kampf: An Analysis.* London: Faber and Faber, 1970.

Mees, Bernard. *The Science of the Swastika.* New York: Central European University Press, 2008.

Michael, Robert. *A Concise History of American Anti-Semitism.* Lanham, MD: Rowman & Littlefield, 2005.

Miyoshi, Tomokazu. *Manji to Tomoe no Kigenko (Thoughts on the Beginning of Manji and Tomoe).* Tokyo: Sanshusha, 1936.

Mori, Sadao. *Bussokuseki o Tazuneru (Visiting Buddha's Footprints).* Kobe, Japan: Bussokuseki Kenkyusho, 1983.

Mosher, Lucinda. *Praying: The Rituals of Faith.* New York: Seabury Books, 2006.

Motwani, Jagat. *None But India (Bharat): The Cradle of Aryans, Sanskrit, Vedas, & Swastika.* Bloomington, IN: iUniverse, 2011.

Mühlberger, Detlef. *Hitler's voice: The Völkischer Beobachter, 1920–1933.* New York: Peter Lang, 2004.

Müller, Friedrich Max. *A History of Ancient Sanskrit Literature.* London: Williams and Norgate, 1859.

_____. *Biographies of Words, and the Home of the Aryas.* London: Longmans, Green & Co., Ltd., 1888

_____. *Dhammapada.* London: Duncan Baird Publishers, 2006.

Müller, Friedrich Max and Cowell, Edward Byles. *Buddhist Mahāyāna Texts.* New York: Cosimo, Inc., 2007.

Nachman, Rebbe of Breslow. *The Empty Chair: Finding Hope and Joy.* Woodstock, NY: Jewish Light Publishing, 1994.

Nagata, Seiji. Translated by John Bester. *Hokusai: Genius of the Japanese Ukiyo-e.* New York: Kodansha, 1995.

Nakamura, Hajime. *Buddha no Shinri no Kotoba, Kanko no Kotoba (Buddha's true words and emotional words).* Tokyo: Iwanami Shoten, 1978.

Newman, Earnest. *The Life of Richard Wagner (v.4).* Cambridge: Cambridge University Press, 1976.

Niwa, Motoji. *Sekai no Bussokuseki (Buddha's Footprints).* Tokyo: Meicho Shuppan, 1992.

O'Brien, Peter. *Beyond the Swastika.* New York: Routledge, 1996.

Oeda, Shiro. *Kamon no Bunkashi (Cutural History of Family Crest).* Tokyo: Kodansha, 1999.

O'Grady, William and Dobrovolsky, Michael. *Contemporary Linguistics: An Introduction.* New York: Longman, 1997.

O'Neill, John. *Night of the Gods, Part 2.* Whitefish, MT: Kessinger Publishing, 2003

Oyama, Kunioki. *Koji o Yuku (Visiting Old Temples): Toshodai-ji, February Issue.* Tokyo: Shogakkan, 2001.

_____. *Koji o Yuku (Visiting Old Temples): Yakushi-ji, April Issue.* Tokyo: Shogakkan, 2001.

Pant, Mohan and Funo, Shuji. *Stupa and Swastika: Historical Urban Planning Principles in Nepal's Kathmandu Valley.* Kyoto: Kyoto University Press, 2007.

Parihar, Subhash. *Some Aspects of Indo-Islamic Architecture.* New Delhi, India: Abhinav Publication, 1999.

Park, Josephine Nock-Hee. *Apparition of Asia: Modernist Form and Asian American Poetics.* Oxford: Oxford University Press, 2008.

Peet, Stephen Denison and Kinnaman, J. O. *The American Antiquarian and Oriental Journal, Volume 26.* Chicago: Jameson & Morse, 1904.

Pennik, Nigel. *The Swastika.* Cambridge, UK: Fenris-Wolf, 1979.

Phillips, Philip and Ford, James A. *Archaeological Survey in the Lower Mississippi Alluvial Valley, 1940–1947.* Tuscaloosa, AL: The University of Alabama Press, 2003.

Poliakov, Leon. *The Aryan Myth.* New York: Basic Books, 1974.

Quinn, Malcolm. *The Swastika: Constructing the Symbol.* New York: Routledge, 1994.

Rausch, David A. *A Legacy of Hatred: Why Christians must not forget the Holocaust.* Grand Rapids, MI: Baker Book House, 1990.

Reitlinger, Gerald. *The Final Solution.* New York: A.S. Barnes, 1961.

Rummel, R.J. *Death by Government.* New Brunswick, NJ: Transaction Publishers, 1994.

Sakamoto, Pamela Rotner. *Japanese Diplomats and Jewish Refugees: A World War II Dilemma.* Westport, CT: Praeger, 1998.

Schliemann, Hendrich. *Ilios, Stadt und land der Trojaner.* Berlin: F.A. Brockhaus, 1881.

_____. *Ilios: The City and Country of the Trojans: The Results of Researchers and Discoveries on the Site of Troy and Throughout the Road in the Years 1871–72–73–78–79.* London: John Murray, Albemarle Street, 1880.

_____. *Troy and its Remains.* London: Murray, 1875.

Scholem, Gershom. *The Messianic Idea in Judaism: And Other Essays on Jewish Spirituality.* New York: Schocken Books, 1971.

Shah, Pravin (JAINA Education Committee Federation of Jain Association in North America). *Jain Philosophy and Practice I.* Gujarat, India: Amrut Graphics, 2002.

_____. *Jainism: Religion of Compassion and Ecology* (revised 2nd Edition). Elmhurst, NY: Federation of Jain Association in North America, 2004.

Shanks, Hershel. *Judaism in Stone.* New York: Harper & Row Publishers, 1979.

Shirer, William L. *The Rise and Fall of the Third Reich: A History of Nazi Germany.* New York-London: Simon & Schuster Paperbacks, 1990.

Sim, David C. and Repschinsk, Boris (Edited). *Matthew and His Christian Contemporaries.* London: T&T Clark, 2008.

Simi, Pete and Futrell, Robert. *American Swastika: Inside the White Power Movement's Hidden Spaces of Hate.* Lanham, MD: Rowman & Littlefield Publishers, 2010.

Singh, Dharam Vir. *Hinduism: An Introduction.* Jaipur, India: Travel Wheels, 1995.

Snodgrass, W. D. *The Fuhrer Bunker: The Compete Cycle: Poems.* Brockport, NY: BOA Editions, 1995.

Stafford, Thomas Albert. *Christian Symbolism in the Evangelical Churches.* Nashville, TN: Abingdon-Cokesbury Press, 1942.

Stain, Leon. *The Racial Thinking of Richard Wagner.* New York: Philosophical Library, 1950.

Steigmann-Gall, Richard. *The Holy Reich: Nazi Conceptions of Christianity. 1919–1945.* New York: Cambridge University Press, 2003.

Stevenson, Sinclair. *The Heart of Jainism.* Oxford: Oxford University Press, 1915.

Tanaka, Yuki. *Hidden Horrors: Japanese War Crimes in World War II.* Boulder, CO: Westview Press⊠, 1997.

Taylor, Telford. *Sword and Swastika; Generals and Nazis in the Third Reich.* New York: Simon & Schuster, 1952.

Tillich, Paul. *The Essential Tillich: An Anthology of the Writings of Paul Tillich.* New York: Macmillan, 1987.

Tillich, Paul (Edited by John P. Clayton). *Main Writings/Hauptwerke Vol. 4: Writings in the Philosophy of Religion.* Berlin: Walter de Gruyter, 1987.

Travers, Chris. The Serpent and the Eagle: An Introduction to the Elder Runic Tradition. Charleston, SC: BookSurge Publishing, 2009.

Uemura, Manji. *Manji no Hakubutsushi* 卍卐の博物誌 *Volume 1.* Kyoto: Koyo Shoten Press, 2008.

_____. *Manji no Hakubutsushi* 卍卐の博物誌 *Volume 2.* Kyoto: Koyo Shoten Press, 2010.

Venugopalan, R. *India: Known Things and Unknown Secrets.* Delhi, India: B. Jain Publishers, 2003.

Wagner, Richard. Translated by William A. Ellis. *Richard Wagner's Prose Works / Vol.3, The Theatre.* London: K. Paul, Trench, Trübner, 1894.

_____. Translated by William A. Ellis. *Richard Wagner's Prose Works / Vol.6, Religion and Art.* London: K. Paul, Trench, Trübner, 1897.

Welch, David. *The Third Reich: Politics and Propaganda.* London: Routledge, 1993.

Whipple, Fred L. *The Mystery of Comets.* Washington, DC: Smithsonian Institute Press, 1985.

Whorf, Benjamin L. *Language, Thought, and Reality [electronic resource]: Selected Writings.* Cambridge, MA: MIT Press, 1964.

Wiener, Peter F. *Martin Luther: Hitler's Spiritual Ancestor.* Parsippany, NJ: American Atheist Press, 1999.

Wiesel, Elie. Translated from the French by Stella Rodway. *Night.* New York: Discus Books, 1960.

Williams, Duncan Ryuken and Moriya, Tomoye. *Issei Buddhism in the Americas.* Champaign, IL: University Illinois Press, 2010.

Wilson, Thomas. *Swastika: The Earliest Known Symbol and Its Migrations* (United States National Museum. Report, 1894). Whitefish, MT: Kessinger Publishing, 1942.

Wistrich, Robert S. *Hitler and the Holocaust.* New York: Modern Library, 2001.

Wulff, Wilhelm. *Zodiac and Swastika.* New York: Coward, McCann & Geoghegan, 1973.

Yenne, Bill. *Hitler's Master of the Dark Arts: Himmler's Black Knights and the Occult Origin of the SS*. Minneapolis, MN: Zenith Imprint, 2010.

Dictionaries and Encyclopedias

Beer, Robert. *The Encyclopedia of Tibetan Symbols and Motifs*. Boston, MA: Shambhala, 1999.

Black, Jeremy A. *Gods, Demons, and Symbols of Ancient Mesopotamia: An Illustrated Dictionary*. London: British Museum Press, 1992.

Canney, Maurice Arthur. *An Encyclopaedia of Religions*. London: George Routledge & Sons, Ltd., 1921.

Charny, Israel W. *Encyclopedia of Genocide*. Santa Barbara, CA: ABC Clio Inc., 1999.

Chikano, Shigeru. *Kamon no Jiten (Dictionary of Family Crest)*. Tokyo: Tokyodo Shuppan, 2008.

Cirlot, J.E. *A Dictionary of Symbols*. New York: Barnes and Noble Books, 1995.

Cooper, Jean C. *An Illustrated Encyclopaedia of Traditional Symbols*. New York: Thames and Hudson, 1978.

Crystal, David. *The Cambridge Encyclopedia of Language*. New York: Cambridge University Press, 1987.

Grimm, Jacob and Grimm, Wilhelm. *Deutsches Worterbuch*. Berlin: Verlag von S. Hirzel, 1877.

Guralink, David B. *Webster's New World Dictionary*. New York: Simon & Schuster, 1984.

Gutman, Israel, ed. *Encyclopedia of the Holocaust*. New York: Macmillan, 1990.

Hagiwara, Unrai. *Bonwa Daijiten (Sanskrit-Japanese Dictionary)*. Tokyo: Kodansha 1978.

Hayashi, Tatsuo and Noda, Matao. *Tetsugaku Jiten (Dictionary of Philosophy)*. Tokyo: Heibonsha, 1971.

Heidtmann, Horst. *Encyclopedia of the Third Reich*. New York: Macmillan, 1991.

Jones, Constance A. and Ryan, James D. *Encyclopedia of Hinduism*. New York: Infobase Publishing, 2007.

Kanemitsu, Jinzaburo. *Sekai Shinboru Daijiten (Encyclopedia of Symbols in the World)*. Tokyo: Daishukan Shoten, 1996.

Katano, Takashi. *Nihon no Danto Monyo Jiten (Dictionary of Traditional Japanese Design)*. Tokyo: Kodansha, 2000.

Koguchi, Iichi and Hori, Ichiro. *Shukyogaku Jiten (Dictionary of Religions)*. Tokyo: Tokyo University Press, 1973.

Landman, Isaak. *The Universal Jewish Encyclopedia*. New York: The Universal Jewish Encyclopedia Inc., 1939–1943.

Laqueur, Walter, ed. *The Holocaust Encyclopedia*. New Haven, CT: Yale University Press, 2001.

Lee, Jonathan H.X. and Nadeau, Kathleen M. *Encyclopedia of Asian American Folklore and Folklife*. Santa Barbara, CA: ABC-Clio, 2010.

Liungman, Carl G. *Dictionary of Symbols*. New York-London: W.W. Norton & Company, 1991.

Michael, Robert and Rosen, Phillip. *Dictionary of Antisemitism from the Earliest Times to the Present*. Lanham, MD: Scarecrow Press, 2007.

Monier-Williams, Monier. *A Sanskrit-English Dictionary*. Oxford: Clarendon Press, 1979.

Morohashi, Tetsuji. *Daikanwa Jiten (The Great Chinese-Japanese Dictionary)*. Tokyo: Daishukan Shoten, 1955.

Murray, James. *A New English Dictionary on Historical Principles*. Oxford: Clarendon Press, 1884.

Nakamura, Hajime. *Bukkyogo Daijiten (Buddhist Terms Dictionary)*. Tokyo: Shoten 1981.

Niwa, Motoji. *Kamon Daizukan (Illustrated Encyclopedia of Family Crest)*. Tokyo: Akita Shoten, 1971.

_____. *Kamon Itsuwa Jiten (Dictionary of Family Crest Stories)*. Tokyo: Rippu Shobo. 1995.

Nosaka, Toshio. *Nihon Kamon Soran (Dictionary of Family Crest in Japan)*. Tokyo: Shin-jinbutsu-Oraisha, 1990.

Okato, Sadaharu. *Moyo no Jiten (Dictionary of Designs)*. Tokyo: Tokyodo Shuppan, 1968.

Ryukoku University. *Bukkyo Daijiten (Encyclopedia of Buddhism)*. Tokyo: Fuzan-bo, 1987.

Sato, Norimasa. *Nippon Kokugo Daijiten (Dictionary of Japanese Language)*. Tokyo: Shogakkan, 2001.

Shinmura, Izuru. *Kojien (Wide Garden of Words)*. Tokyo: Iwanami Books, 1998.

Simpson, J.A. and Weiner, E.S.C. *The Oxford English Dictionary (Second Edition)*. Oxford: Clarendon Press, 1989.

Smith, Jonathan Z. *The Harper Collins Dictionary of Religion*. New York: Harper Collins Publisher, 1995.

Snyder, Louis L. *Encyclopedia of The Third Reich*. London: Robert Hale, 1976.

Speake, Jennifer. *The Dent Dictionary of Symbols in Christian Art*. London: Dent and Sons, 1994.

Sewell, Robert. *Notes on the Swastika*. Oxford: Oxford University Press, 1881.

Taylor, James and Shaw, Warren. *Dictionary of The Third Reich*. London, England: Penguin Books, 1997.

Ueda, Mannen and Okada, Masayuki. *Daijiten (Dictionary of Characters)*. Tokyo: Kodansha, 1965.

Willis, Bruce W. *The Adinkra Dictionary: A Visual Primer on The Language of ADINKRA*. Washington DC: The Pyramid Complex, 1998.

Woolf, Henry B. *Webster's New Collegiate Dictionary*. Springfied, MA: G. & C. Merriam Company, 1973.

Yamashita, K. *Imeji, Shimboru Jiten (Dictionary of Images and Symbols)*. Tokyo: Daishukan Shhoten, 1984.

Zentner, Christian and Bedurftig, Friedemann. *The Encyclopedia of the Third Reich*. New York: Macmillan Publishing Company, 1991.

大正新修大蔵経 (Taisho-Edition Buddhist Sutras, *Taisho Daizokyo*). Tokyo: Daizo Shuppan, 1935.

Magazines and Booklets

Carus, Paul. "Fylfot and Swastika," *The Open Court* 1902: issue 3. London: Open Court Publishing Co, 1902. 356–366.

Clement, Ernest. "Cross in Japanese Heraldry," *The Open Court* 1899: issue 12. London: Open Court Publishing Co, 1902, 742–746.

Crawfurd, John. "Notes on Sir Charles Antiquity of Man," *Anthropological Review*. Royal Anthropological Institute of Great Britain and Ireland, 1864–1870, 173–174.

Elbogen, Greta. Remember Me! A Collection of Poems by Greta Elbogen. Self-published 2008 and 2012.

Guardian, Manchester. "Cross and swastika," *Friends of Europe Publications: no. 28*. London: Friends of Europe, 1935. 7–17.

Jones, William, Sir. "Third Anniversary Discourse," *Asiatick Researches Vol. 1*. London and New York: Routledge, 2000 (first published in Calcutta, 1788), 415–431.

Lal, B. B. "Aryan Invasion of India: Perpectuation of a myth," *The Indo-Aryan Controversy: Evidence and Inference in Indian History*. New York: Routledge, 2005, 50–74.

Manns, William. "The Most Misunderstood Mark," *American Cowboy*. El Segundo, CA: Active Interest Media, Nov–Dec 2000, 84–86.

Metspalu, Mait and Romero, Irene Gallego. "Shared and Unique Components of Human Population Structure and Genome-Wide Signals of Positive Selection in South Asia," *The American Journal of Human Genetics*. Bethesda, MD: AJHG, December 9, 2011, 731–744.

Parker, William Thornton. "The Swastika: A Prophetic Symbol," *The Open Court* 1907: Iss. 9. London: Open Court Publishing Co, 1907, 539–546.

Rabbow, Arnold. *Shrwartz-Rot-Gold: Einheit in Freiheit*. Berlin: Der Flaggenkurier Nr. 25, 2007, 41–45.

Weinel, Heinrich. "Richard Wagner and Christianity," *The American Journal of Theology Vol 7, No. 4*. Chicago, IL: The University of Chicago Press, October,1903, 609–634.

World Council of Religious Leaders OF The Millennium World Peace Summit. *Report of the 2nd Hindu-Jewish Leadership Summit.* February 17–20, 2008.

DVDs

Cohen, Peter. *Architecture of Doom (Undergangens arkitektur).* 1989.

Hamburg–Deutsche Grammophon. *Siegfried.* Music and libretto by Richard Wagner. 1990.

Jacoby, Oren. *Sister Rose's Passion.* 2004.

Metropolitan Opera. *Die Walkure: Wagner's "Ring" at the MET.* 1989.

Riefenstahl, Leni. *Triumph of the Will (German: Triumph des Willens).* 1935.

Websites

http://en.auschwitz.org.pl

http://healingandhope2011.com

http://reclaimtheswastika.com

http://rexcurry.blogspot.com

http://svasticross.blogspot.com

http://www.etymonline.com

http://www.janm.org

http://www.jhi.pl

http://www.stephen-knapp.com

http://www.ushmm.org

http://www.youtube.com/watch?v=V442lxwRvYA

Endnotes

1   Greta Elbogen, *Remember Me! A Collection of Poems by Greta Elbogen*, 2nd Edition (self-published, 2012).

2   Rebbe Nachman of Breslow. *The Empty Chair: Finding Hope and Joy* (Woodstock: Jewish Light Publishing, 1994), 15, 29, 77, 78, 79 and 112.

3   *The War Against the Jews: 1933–1945* by Lucy S. Dawidowicz (Bantam, 1986) who is an American historian shows 5,933,900 deaths of Jews listing from various countries. *Atlas of the Holocaust* by Martin Gilbert (New York: Pergamon Press, 1988) who is a British historian also estimated just under six millions.

4   http://www.cbsnews.com/news/hundreds-of-graves-desecrated-at-jewish-cemetery-in-france/, http://edition.cnn.com/2015/02/18/europe/france-cemeteries-vandalized/index.html (accessed on February 26, 2015).

5   http://jpupdates.com/2015/02/24/montreal-swastikas-spray-painted-cars-underground-parking-lot/ (accessed on February 26, 2015).

6   http://www.utsandiego.com/news/2015/feb/23/swastikas-hate-graffiti-sprayed-at-san-diego-high/ (accessed on February 26, 2015).

7   http://www.dailymail.co.uk/news/article-2958874/Idiot-vandals-target-Hindu-temple-spray-painting-swastika-despite-sign-sacred-symbol.html (accessed on February 26, 2015).

8   Rebbe Nachman of Breslow. *The Empty Chair: Finding Hope and Joy* (Woodstock: Jewish Light Publishing, 1994), 29.

9   A photo of a similar flower shrine is found in Fig. 85 (Fresno Buddhist Temple Hanamatsuri).

10 "Bejeweled in Greenpoint, Brooklyn Slammed for Selling Swastika Look-Alike Earrings," *New York Daily News* (January. 10, 2012).

11 *Report of the Hindu-Jewish Leadership Summit* (February 17–20, 2008), 9.

12 Yuki Tanaka, *Hidden Horrors: Japanese War Crimes in World War II* (Boulder, CO: Westview Press, 1997), 111–125

13 For example, in the case of "Rape of Nanking," the estimated total killed varies: 40,000 dead by Arthur Zich; 100,000 by Dick Wilson; 260,000 by chief prosecutor of the District Court of Nanking; 300,000 by official Chinese figure; 200,000 is estimated by R.J. Rummel. R.J. Rummel, *Death by Government* (New Brunswick, N.J: Transaction Publishers 1994), 145.

14 Israel W. Charny, *Encyclopedia of Genocide: Vol. 1* (Santa Barbara, CA: ABC Clio Inc., 1999), 27.

15 Mr. Koji Kobayashi shared his personal experience of the Hiroshima bombing at the annual "Interfaith Peace Gathering to Commemorate Hiroshima & Nagasaki Atomic Bombings" on August 5, 2006. It was the first time that he joined this peace event in Manhattan.

16 United States Holocaust Memorial Museum site provides various excellent resources: http://www.ushmm.org

17 The author interviewed Greta Elbogen in Manhattan, New York, on December 20, 2011.

18 W.D. Snodgrass, *The Fuhrer Bunker: The Compete Cycle: Poems* (Brockport, NY: BOA Editions, 1995), 11.

19 An official topographic map of Japan was standardized in 1884 by Meiji government.

20 Professor Uemura's name is written as "植村卍" in Japanese characters.

21 Ernest Clement, "Cross in Japanese Heraldry," *The Open Court* 1899, issue 12 (Winter, 1899), 745–746.

22 http://www.city.hirosaki.aomori.jp/ (accessed on January 12, 2012).

23 http://www.shorinjikempo.or.jp/wsko/report/65.html (accessed on November 11, 2012).

24 *Pokemon Symbol A Swastika?* The Associated Press November 1999, www.theescapist.com/ pokemon5.htm (accessed on October 20, 2012).

25 Ibid.

26 For example, Animation from "Bleach #436," *Weekly Shonen Jump magazine*, http://www.mangareader. net/bleach/436/23 (accessed on January 14, 2012).

27 Dave Chipps, edit, "About the translation" from *Blade of Immortal* (Dark Horse Comics. Inc.2010).

28 Seiji Nagata, translated by John Bester. *Hokusai: Genius of the Japanese Ukiyo-e* (Tokyo, New York: Kodansha, 1995), 52.

29 『新形小紋帳』(*Notes of New Shapes and Small Patterns*) published in 1824.

30 Ian Buruma, "Fatal Attractions," *New York Times* (February 13, 1994).

31 Translation from original Japanese by the author.

32 *Kojien* (Tokyo: Iwanami Books, 1998), s.v. "Manji."

33 *Nippon Kokugo Daijiten* (Tokyo: Shogakkan, 2001), s.v. "Manji."

34 *Daikanwa Jiten* (Tokyo: Daishukan Shoten, 1955), s.v. "Manji."

35 *Daijiten* (Tokyo: Kodansha, 1965), s.v. "Manji."

36 *Bonwa Daijiten* (Tokyo: Kodansha 1978), s.v. "Manji."

37 *Bukkyogo Daijiten* (Tokyo: Tokoyo Shoten 1981), s.v. "Manji."

38 According to *Bukkyo Daijiten* (Toyama-bo, 1987), the svastika was first officially used as a Chinese character in 639 (長寿2年) during the time of Empress Wu Zetian (則天武后) in China.

39   According to the *Kojien* (Tokyo: Iwanami Books, 1998), [hakenkreuz German] is translated as hook-cross. It comes from the same origin of the manji, and is a right turn hook, that is 卐. This sign was used by the Nazi party's flag from 1919, and became the German national flag from 1935 to 1945.

40   According to the *Kojien* (Tokyo: Iwanami Books, 1998), [kagi juji] the translation of Hakenkreuz.

41   Translation of various sutras from original Chinese by the author.

42   「胸有萬字」『長阿含經』*Agama Sutra* (Taisho Daizokyo volume 1, 1935), 5;「胸有卍字」『佛說普曜經』*Sutra on Universal Day* (TD vol. 3), 496;「胸有万字」『佛說太子瑞應本起經』*Sutra on the Prince's Magnificent Life* (TD vol. 3), 474;「胸有萬字」『大薩遮尼乾子所說經』*Sutra on the Discourse by Mahāsatyanirgrantha* (TD vol. 9), 345;「胸表卍字」『無量義經』*Sutra of Immeasurable Meanings* (TD vol. 9), 385;「胸摽卍字」『大方廣佛華嚴經』*Garland Sutra* (TD vol. 10), 349;「胸萬字相」『佛說十地經』*Sutra on the Ten Stages* (TD vol. 10), 535;「胸有卍字」『優婆夷淨行法門經』*Sutra on the Dharma-gate of Pure Practice* (TD vol. 14), 955;「胸德字萬字」『禪祕要法經』*Sutra on the Essential Dharma of Zen* (TD vol. 15), 255;「示胸卍字」『佛說觀佛三昧海經』*Ocean-like Sutra on Samadhi through Meditation on the Buddha* (TD vol. 15), 685;「佛胸上卍字」『陀羅尼集經』*Sutra on the Collection of Dhāraṇī* (TD vol. 15), 870;「胸前作於卍字」『不空羂索陀羅尼經』*Dhāraṇī Sutra of Amogha Paaza* (TD vol. 20), 415.

43   「童子髮圓而右旋状如万字」『佛本行集經』*Sutra of the Collection of the Original Acts of the Buddha* (TD vol. 3), 696.

44   「指萬字千輻輪相」『佛本行集經』*Sutra of the Collection of the Original Acts of the Buddha* (TD vol. 3), 736;「指端各生卍字」『佛說觀佛三昧海經』*Ocean-like Sutra on Samadhi through Meditation on the Buddha* (TD vol. 15), 649.

45   「髮有五卍字」『方廣大莊嚴經』*Sutra of the Great Adornments* (TD vol. 3), 557.

46   「萬字輪文。福德之手」『佛本行集經』*Sutra of the Collection of the Original Acts of the Buddha* (TD vol. 3, 705);「菩薩舉萬字福相百千威德之手。作無畏印」『佛說衆許摩訶帝經』卷第五 *Sutra of Sanghabhedavastu* (TD vol. 3), 946.

47   「兩足下兩手中兩肩上項中皆滿字相分明」『過去現在因果經』*Sutra of Causes from Past and Present* (TD vol. 3), 627;『摩訶般若波羅蜜經』*Great Prajna Paramita Sutra* (TD vol. 8), 395.

48   「萬字現佛徳現天下」『修行本起經』*Sutra of the Practice and Original Raising* (TD vol. 3), 464.

49   「胸有萬字示功德相」『大薩遮尼乾子所說經』*Sutra on the Discourse by Mahāsatyanirgrantha* (TD vol. 9), 345

50   「表裏皆有吉祥之相卍」『大寶積經』*Great Jewel-Heap Sutra* (TD vol. 11), 109.

51   「於萬字印中。說佛八萬四千諸功德行」『佛說觀佛三昧海經』*Ocean-like Sutra on Samadhi through Meditation on the Buddha* (TD vol. 15), 661.

52   「万字名實相印。諸佛如來無量無邊阿僧祇劫學得此印。得此印故不畏生死。不染五欲」『佛說觀佛三昧海經』*Ocean-like Sutra on Samadhi through Meditation on the Buddha* (TD vol. 15), 665.

53   The Chinese character for the swastika also means "full."

54 「滿字者乃是一切善法言説之根本也。譬如世間爲惡行者名爲半人。修善行者名爲滿人」『大般涅槃經』 *Great Nirvana Sutra* (TD vol. 12), 655.

55 「胸前自然卍字大人相」『寶女所問經』 *Sutra of the Precious Woman's Questions* (TD vol. 13), 469.

56 「得大人相胸有卍字」『優婆夷淨行法門經』 *Sutra on the Dharma-Gate of Pure Practice.* (TD vol. 14), 958.

57 「於卍字金剛莊嚴心藏中放大光明」『大方廣佛華嚴經』 *Garland Sutra* (TD vol. 10), 310.

58 「即時如來從胸卍字涌出寶光。其光晃昱有百千色。十方微塵普佛世界一時周遍」『大佛頂如來密因修證了義諸菩薩萬行首楞嚴經』 *Sutra of Śūraṅgama.* (TD vol. 19), 109.

59 「見佛胸相光者。除却十二万億劫生死之罪」『佛説觀佛三昧海經』 *Ocean-like Sutra on Samadhi through Meditation on the Buddha* (TD vol. 15), 665.

60 J.C. Cooper, *An Illustrated Encyclopedia of Traditional Symbols* (New York: Thames and Hudson, 1978), 165–166.

61 「世尊甚奇特。但於胸字説無量義。何況佛心所有功德」『佛説觀佛三昧海經』 *Ocean-like Sutra on Samadhi through Meditation on the Buddha* (TD vol. 15), 661.

62 「當以滿字入菩薩之心」『大毘盧遮那佛説要略念誦經』 *Sutra Taught by Great Virocana Buddha about Essence and Summery of Meditation and Chanting.* (TD vol. 18). 60.

63 *Sukhavativyuha Sutra (Sutra of the Buddha of Immeasurable Life)*, translated from Sanskrit by Max Muller, *Buddhist Mahāyāna Texts* (New York: Cosimo, Inc., 2007), 50.

64 「若爲十方諸佛速來授手者。當於數珠手。若爲成就一切上妙梵音聲者。當於寶鐸手。若爲口業辭辯巧妙者。當於寶印手。若爲善神龍王常來擁護者。當於俱尸鐵鉤手」『千手千眼觀世音菩薩廣大圓滿無礙大悲心陀羅尼經』 *Dhāraṇī Sutra of the Great Compassionate Avalokitesvara* (TD vol. 20), 111.

65 「卍字之文　梵云室哩二合末蹉倉何反　唐云吉祥相也有　云萬字者謬説也非是字也乃是如來身上數處　有此吉祥之文　大福德之相」『一切経音義』 *Meanings on the Sound of All the Sutras* (TD vol. 54), 378.

66 「萬字者。表無漏性德。梵云阿悉底迦。此云有樂。即是吉祥勝德之相。有此相者。必受安樂。則天長壽二年。權制此字。安於天樞。其形如此。」『首楞嚴義疏注經』 *Commentary on the Śūraṅgama Samādhi Sutra* (TD vol. 39), 841.

67 「標卍相。表萬德吉祥。内智契如名金剛界」『大方廣佛華嚴經疏』 *Commentary on the Avatamsaka Sutra* (TD vol. 35), 715.

68 「卍字正翻爲吉祥海」『大方廣佛華嚴經疏』 *Commentary on the Avatamsaka Sutra* (TD vol. 35), 866.

69 「胸有卍字名實相印。放大光明」『往生要集』 *Collections of the Essentials for Rebirth* (TD vol. 84), 54.

70 「胸前卍字中出無數百千億阿脩羅王。皆悉示現不可思議自在幻力。令百千世界皆大震動者。胸是勇猛義卍者清涼義故。於中出修羅衆。表精勤勇猛震動摧破煩惱魔軍」『新華嚴經論』 *Treatise on the New Translation of the Flower Ornament Scripture* (TD vol. 36), 961.

71 「菩薩。於功德莊嚴金剛萬字胸出一大光明名壞魔怨。有十阿僧祇百千光明以爲眷屬。出已悉照十方無量世界。示無量神力亦來入是大菩薩功德莊嚴金剛萬字胸」『十地經論』 *Treatise on the Ten Stages Sutra* (TD vol. 26), 195.

72 Robert Beer, *The Encyclopedia of Tibetan Symbols and Motifs* (Boston: Shambhala 1999), 344.

73 J.C. Cooper, *An Illustrated Encyclopedia of traditional Symbols* (New York: Thames and Hudson, 1978), 166.

74 Thomas Wilson, *Swastika: The Earliest Known Symbol and Its Migrations* (United States National Museum. Report, 1894) (Whitefish, MT: Kessinger Publishing, 1942), 904, 905.)

75 F.W. Dillistone, *The Power of Symbols in Religion and Culture.* (London: SCM Press, 1986), 123.

76 Ibid.

77 Paul Tillich, *Main Writings/Hauptwerke Vol. 4: Writings in the Philosophy of Religion* (Berlin: Walter de Gruyter, 1987), 416.

78 「如人以指指月以示惑者。惑者視指而不視月」『大智度論』*Treatise on Great Wisdom Salvation* (Taisho Daizokyo vol. 25), 125.

79 Robert Beer, *The Encyclopedia of Tibetan Symbols and Motifs* (Boston: Shambhala 1999), 344.

80 J.C. Cooper, *An Illustrated Encyclopedia of Traditional Symbols* (New York: Thames and Hudson, 1978), 166.

81 Figure 39: Dr. M.G. Prasad showed me a book published in India, and explained the picture on the book as follows. "A Kalasha (sacred vessel) that is filled with water mixed with materials namely saffron and cardamom. A coconut is placed on the top with mango leaves. The water is sanctified with chanting of Veda Mantras. The seven holy rivers such as Ganga, Yamuna, etc, are invoked. This Kalasha is used on special occasions of sacraments and rituals. The Sacred water is used for rituals and also sprinkled around the house to sanctify and also used for taking bath. The use of OM and Swastika is also for sanctification."

82 *Asana* means "sitting down.'"

83 Stephen Knapp, "Basic Points about Vedic Culture / Hinduism" from http://www.stephen-knapp.com/basic_points_about_vedic_culture_hinduism.htm (accessed on January 10, 2012).

84 India 5 Rupees commemorative coin Bhagwan Mahavir, issued by the Government of India in 2001, which was given to the author by Naresh Jain, who owns the envelope with the Jain symbol stamp.

85 Pravin Shah, *JAINISM–Religions of Compassion and Ecology* (Federation of Jain Association in North America, 2004), 30.

86 J.C. Cooper, *An Illustrated Encyclopedia of Traditional Symbols* (New York: Thames and Hudson, 1978), 166.

87   *Encyclopedia of Hinduism* (New York: Infobase Publishing, 2007), 448.

88   Sinclair Stevenson, *The Heart of Jainism* (Forgotten Books, 1915), 53.

89   John E. Cort, *Jains in the World: Religious Values and Ideology in India* (Oxford University Press, 2001), 194.

90   Isaak Landman, *The Universal Jewish Encyclopedia: Volume 10* (New York: The Universal Jewish encyclopedia, inc., 1939–1943), 111.

91   Joseph Gutmann, *Iconography of Religions: Judaism. The Jewish Sanctuary* (BRILL, 1983), 21.

92   Gershom Scholem, *The Star of David: History of a Symbol. The Messianic Idea in Judaism: And Other Essays on Jewish Spirituality* (New York: Schocken Books, 1971), 260.

93   http://historyhuntersinternational.org/2010/05/19/archaeology-of-ein-gedi/ (accessed on January 12, 2012).

94   http://en.epochtimes.com/news/7-2-16/51803.html (accessed on January 12, 2012).

95   Thomas Wilson, *Swastika: The Earliest Known Symbol and Its Migrations* (United States National Museum. Report, 1894), 767.

96   Paul Carus, "Fylfot and Swastika," from *The Open Court* 1902: issue 3 (London: Open Court Publishing Co, 1902), 359.

97   Jennifer Speake, *The Dent Dictionary of Symbols in Christian Art* (London: J. M. Dent Ltd. 1994), 134.

98   Paul Carus, "Fylfot and Swastika" from *The Open Court* (London: Open Court Publishing Co, 1902), 359.

99   William Parker. *The Swastika: A Prophetic Symbol.* From The Open Court, Volume 21 (London: Open Court Publishing Co, 1907), 545.

100 Ibid., 541.

101 Bronze effigy on the tomb of Bishop Huyshe Wolcott Yeatman-Biggs, first bishop of Coventry Cathedral, England. Sculptor William Hamo Thornycroft, 1924. Restored by E. Roland Bevan, 1951. The tomb survived the destruction of the old cathedral by the Blitz in 1940 and still stands on its original site in the cathedral ruins.

102 "Byzantine Swastika": http://www.youtube.com/watch?v=V442lxwRvYA (accessed on January 12, 2012).

103 "Europe's 'Oldest Swastika' Unearthed." *Daily and Sunday Express*, May 25, 2010.

104 Joseph Campbell, *Flight of the Wild Gander, Explorations in the Mythological Dimension* (New World Library, 2002), 117.

105 Getnet Tamene, *Features of the Ethiopian Orthodox Church and Clergy* (Asian and African Studies, 1998), 93.

106 http://www.crystallography.fr/mathcryst/pdf/istanbul/Necefoglu_slides.pdf (accessed on August 31, 2013).

107 J.C. Cooper, *An Illustrated Encyclopedia of Traditional Symbols* (New York: Thames and Hudson, 1978), 166.

108 Article "Application of the Swastika in Mughal Architecture of India," from website: http://www.anistor.gr/english/enback/e053.htm (accessed on January 16, 2012).

109 Chris Travers, *The Serpent and the Eagle: An Introduction to the Elder Runic Tradition* (Charleston, SC: BookSurge Publishing, 2009), 12.

110 Bruce Willis, *The Adinkra Dictionary* (Washington DC: The Pyramid Complex, 1998), 142.

111 Thomas Wilson, *Swastika: The Early Known Symbol and Its Migrations* (United States National Museum. Report, 1894), 879–925.

112 Philip Phillips, and James A Ford, *Archaeological Survey in the Lower Mississippi Alluvial Valley, 1940–1947* (University of Alabama Press, 2003), 132,160,496, 522. The survey reported that the most common design elements found were the spiral meander and swastika spiral.

113 Frank Water, *Book of the Hopi* (New York: Penguin Books, 1963), 35, 114.

114 William Manns, "Most Most Misunderstood Mark," *American Cowboy* (Active Interest Media, Inc. Nov–Dec 2000), 84–86.

115 Alison R. Bernstein, *American Indians and World War II: Toward a New Era in Indian Affairs* (University of Oklahoma Press, 1999), 20 (reads from the photo).

116 "Swastika" Black Brook, NY 12985 (Clinton County, NY) The "swastika" post office opened in 1913 and closed in 1958.

117 ManWoman, *Gentle Swastika* (Cranbrook, BC: Flyfoot Press: 2001), 31–34.

118 http://www.iowadot.gov/autotrails/autoroutes.htm (accessed on January 12, 2012).

119 John Howard, *Concentration Camps on the Home Front: Japanese Americans in the House of Jim Crow* (University of Chicago Press, 2008), 162.

120 Duncan Ryuken Williams and Tomoye Moriya, *Issei Buddhism in the Americas* (University Illinois Press, 2010), 137.

121 Tetsuden Kashima, *Buddhism in America* (Westport, Conn; Greenwood Press, 1977), 115.

122 Josephine Nock-Hee Park, *Apparition of Asia: Modernist form and Asian American Poetics* (Oxford University Press, 2008), 101.

123 Lawson Fusao Inaba, *Only What We Could Carry: The Japanese American Internment Experience* (Berkeley: Heyday Books, 2000]), 171.

124 The Japanese American Museum now occupies the space of the former Nishi Hongwan-ji Los Angeles Betsuin Buddhist temple.

125 Adolf Hitler, translated by Ralph Manheim, *Mein Kampf* (Boston: Houghton Mifflin, 1943), 495–496. I used Manheim's translation unless specified.

126 Arnold Rabbow, *Shrwartz-Rot-Gold: Einheit in Freiheit* (Der Flaggenkurier Nr.25, 2007), 41–45.

127 Adolf Hitler, translated by Ralph Manheim, *Mein Kampf* (Boston: Houghton Mifflin, 1943), 496–97.

128 Ibid., 492, 495.

129 Ibid., 492.

130 Ibid., 496.

131 Werner Maser, *Hitler's Mein Kampf: An Analysis* (London: Faber and Faber, 1970), 79.

132 Joachim C. Fest, *Hitler* (New York: Harcourt Brace Jovanovich, 1974), 36.

133 Ostara III, 1 (1930), iv. Later Lanz used the "Kruckenkreuz" (crutch cross or cross potent) symbol which is the combined symbol of right turn and left turn swastikas.

卐 + 卐 ➔ ╬

134 Guido von List, *Das Geheimnis der Runen* (Leipzig, Germany: E. F. Steinacker, 1938), 20.

135 Michael Marrus (Ed.), *The Nazi Holocaust–Part 2: The Origins of the Holocaust* (Westport, CT: Meckler Corporation, 1989), 92.

136 Carl Liungman, *Dictionary of Symbols* (New York: W.W. Norton & Company, 1991), 67.

137 German version was taken from *Mein Kampf*, München: Zentralverlag der NSDAP, Frz. Eher Nachf, 1940. "In the swastika (we see) the mission of the struggle for the **victory** of the Aryan man, and, by the same token, the **victory** of the idea of creative work, which as such always has been and always will be anti-Semitic."

138 Heinrich Schliemann, *Troy and its Remains* (London: Murray, 1875), 102.

139 Bristol Blenheim BL-129 of ValokLtue Ahtiainen (1939–43).

140 William Thornton Parker, *The Swastika: A Prophetic Symbol* (Open Court, 1907), 541.

141 Adolf Hitler, *Sämtliche Aufzeichnungen: 1905–1924* (Stuttgart, Deutsche: Verlags-Anstalt, 1980), 185–186. English translation is by Hasso Castrup. The author changed the word "Swastika" to "Hakenkreuz" in English translation to emphasize the original German.

142 Four noble truths: 1) truth of suffering; 2) truth of cause of suffering ; 3) truth of ceasing the cause of suffering; 4) truth of paths to cease the suffering.

143 All emphasis is the author's.

144 Translation from the Pali texts by Thanissaro Bhikkhu, an American Theravada Buddhist monk of the Dhammayut Order, Thai forest kammatthana tradition. He is currently the abbot of Metta Forest Monastery in San Diego.

145 Translated by the author.

146 Translation by Daw Mya Tin, M.A. *The Dhammapada*: Verses and Stories Editorial Committee, Burma Tipitaka Association Rangoon, Burma, 1986.

147 *The Dhammapada*, Chapter XIV "The Buddha (The Awakened)," Verse 190, 191.

148 Ibid., Chapter II "On Earnestness," Verse 21, 22.

149 Ibid., Chapter VI "The Wise Man (Pandita)," Verse 79.

150 Ibid., Chapter XII "Self." Verse 164.

151   Ibid., Chapter XVIII "Impurity." Verse 236.

152   Ibid., Chapter XIX "The Just." Verse. 270.

153   Sir William Jones, "Third Anniversary Discourse," *Asiatick Researches Vol. 1* (London and New York: Routledge 2000, First published in Calcutta, 1788), 422.

154   Max Muller, *A History of Ancient Sanskrit Literature* (London: Williams and Norgate, 1859), 11–12.

155   In 1888, Max Muller emphatically insisted "Aryan" did not refer to race. "I have declared again and again that if I say Aryans, I mean neither blood nor bones, nor hairs nor skull; I mean simply those who speak an Aryan language," he said. Friedrich Max Muller, *Biographies of Words, and the Home of the Aryas* (London: Longmans, Green & Co., Ltd., 1888), 89.

156   Current linguists agree to use the term "(Proto) Indo-European language."

157   Charles Lyell, *Geological Evidences of the Antiquity of Man.* (London: Murray, 1863), 354.

158   John Crawfurd, "Notes on Sir Charles Antiquity of Man" from *Anthropological Review* (Royal Anthropological Institute of Great Britain and Ireland, 1864–1870), 173, 174.

159   B.B. Lal, *India 1947–1997: New Light on the Indus Civilization* (New Delhi: Aryan Books International, 1998), 116–123.

160   Mait Metspalu and Irene Gallego Romero etc., "Shared and Unique Components of Human Population Structure and Genome-Wide Signals of Positive Selection in South Asia," *American Journal of Human Genetics* (Bethesda, MD:, December 9, 2011), 731–744.

161   Dr. Henry Schliemann, *Ilios: The City and Country of the Trojans* (London: John Murray, Albemarle Street,1880), 348.

162   Thomas Wilson, *Swastika: The Earliest Known Symbol and Its Migrations* (United States National Museum. Report, 1894), 770–780.

163   Robert Philips Greg, *On the Meaning and Origin of the Fylfot and Swastika* (Westminster: Nichols and Sons, 1884), 33.

164   Nicholas Goodrick-Clarke, *Hitler's Priestess: Savitri Devi, the Hindu-Aryan Myth, and Neo-Nazism* (New York: New York University Press, 1998), 33–34.

165   "Volk": people, nation. "Geist": spirit.

166   Louis L. Snyder, *Encyclopedia of the Third Reich* (London: Robert Hale, 1976), 277.

167   Like Hitler, Chamberlain also idolized Wagner, and was married to Wagner's daughter Eva. Hitler and Chamberlain met in 1923, and a letter written from Chamberlain to Hitler in 1924 expressed Hitler's destiny to rule Germany.

168   Houston Stewart Chamberlain, *Foundation of the Nineteenth Century* (Munchen: F. Bruckmann, 1911), xx.

169   *Mein Kampf,* 290.

170   Ibid.

171   Ibid., 293.

172 Ibid., 290.

173 Ibid., 291.

174 Ibid., 297.

175 Ibid., 299.

176 Ibid., 291.

177 Ibid., 294.

178 Ibid., 295.

179 Ibid., 297.

180 Ibid., 286.

181 Ibid., 296.

182 Ibid., 300.

183 Ibid., 427.

184 Ibid., 447.

185 Ibid., 561.

186 *Hitler's Master of the Dark Arts: Himmler's Black Knights and the Occult Origin of the SS* by Bill Yenne (Minneapolis, MN: Zenith Imprint, 2010), 143–146. See further details in Christopher Hale, *Himmler's Crusade: The Nazi Expedition to Find the Origins of the Aryan Race* (Hoboken, N.J.: John Wiley & Sons, 2003).

187 *Mein Kampf*, 497.

188 Houston Stewart Chamberlain, *Foundation of the Nineteenth Century* (Munchen: F. Bruckmann, 1911), 249.

189 Ibid., 205.

190 Ibid., 211.

191 Figure 99, D.N.S.A.P=Danmarks Nationalsocialistiske Arbejderparti (National Socialist Workers' Party of Denmark) is the largest Nazi party in Denmark.

192 http://news.google.com/ newspapers?nid=1946&dat=19411024&id=CIAuAAAAIBAJ&sjid=3ZgF AAAAIBAJ&pg=5597,4411225 (accessed on August 25, 2013). End of All Christian Churches Mapped in New German Program, *Montreal Gazette*, October 24, 1941.

193 Though small in number, there were Catholics as well as Protestants who opposed Hitler's regime. A group of Protestants including Martin Niemoller, Karl Barth, and Dietrich Bonhoeffer who were opposed to the Nazis were known as the "Confessional Church."

194 Walter Laqueur, ed., *The Holocaust Encyclopedia* (New Haven: Yale University Press, 2001), 427.

195 John Conway, *The Nazi Persecution of the Churches, 1933–1945* (New York: Basic Books, 1968), 364–365. Appendix 9: A Christmas Sermon 1936 preached in Solingen (Source: file of the Old Prussian Union Church, Berlin). The translation cited above uses the term "swastika," although the original German text uses the word "Hakenkreuz." In the above quote I have changed it back to the original.

This passage was by an unknown author found in the files of Old Prussian Union Church in Berlin.

196 Avner Falk, *Anti-Semitism: A History and Psychoanalysis of Contemporary Hatred* (Westport, CT: Praeger Publishers, 2008), 21. The German word *antisemitisch* was first used in 1860 by Moritz Steinschneider.

197 *Mein Kampf*, 497. Author has substituted Hook-Cross for "Swastika"

198 There are many resources written about Christian anti-Semitism in European history from simple descriptions such as United States Holocaust Memorial Museum website to detailed studies such as Phyllis Goldstein, *A Convenient Hatred: The History of Antisemitism* (Brookline, MA; Facing History and Ourselves, 2011); Walter Laqueur, *The Changing Face of Anti-Semitism: From Ancient Times to the Present Day* (New York; Oxford University Press, 2006); David Nirenberg, *Anti-Judaism: The Western Tradition* (New York: W. W. Norton & Company, 2014); David Berger *History and Hate: The Dimensions of Anti-Semitism* (Philadelphia, PA: Jewish Publication Society, 1986); William Nicholls, *Christian Antisemitism: A History of Hate* (Lanham, MD: Rowman & Littlefield, 1995); Thomas Asbridge, *The First Crusade: A New History* (New York: Oxford University Press, 2005

199 The expression "the Jews" appears 79 times in the John's Gospel, on the other hands, 5 times each in Matthew and Luke, and 6 times in Mark. David C. Sim and Boris Repschinsk (edited), *Matthew and His Christian Contemporaries* (London: T&T Clark, 2008), 67.

200 Albert of Aachen, edited and translated Susan B. Edgington, *Albert of Aachen: Historia Ierosolimitana, History of the Journey to Jerusalem* (New York: Oxford University Press, 2007), 53.

201 Two translations are available *The Jews and Their Lies* from Liberty Bell Publications and *On the Jews and Their Lies* from lulu.com. Here I use the latter *On the Jews and Their Lies* which is a less censored version. It is translated by Martin H. Bertram.

202 *Mein Kampf*, 65.

203 Ibid., 52.

204 Ibid., 56.

205 Ibid., 55.

206 Ibid.

207 Ibid., 98.

208 Ibid., 213.

209 Adolf Hitler, *Sämtliche Aufzeichnungen: 1905–1924* (Stuttgart, Deutsche: Verlags-Anstalt, 1980), 1032.

210 Bishops of the Evangelical Lutheran Church of America gathered in Chicago and officially renounced Martin Luther's anti-Semitic writings in November 1994.

211 A letter written by Pastor Riechelmann to a German newspaper on the Jewish Question (from the *Oldenburgischen Rundschreiben*, 7 October 1935). David A.

Rausch, *A Legacy of Hatred: Why Christians Must Not forget the Holocaust* (Grand Rapids, MI: Baker Book House, 1990), 167.

212 James Caroll, *Constantines's Sword* (Boston, MA: Houghton Mifflin, 2001), 428.

213 The correct section is John 8:39.

214 Martin Luther, *On the Jews and Their Lies* (USA: Lulu.com, 2011), 4.

215 Adolf Hitler, Translated by James Murphy, *Mein Kampf* (London: Hutchison & Co., 1939), 30.

216 Ibid., 152

217 *On the Jews and Their Lies*, 31.

218 Ibid., 107.

219 Translated by James Murphy, *Mein Kampf*, 196.

220 *On the Jews and Their Lies*, 111.

221 Ibid., 114.

222 Susannah Heschel, *The Aryan Jesus: Christian Theologians and the Bible in Nazi Germany* (Princeton University Press, 2008), 1.

223 *On the Jews and Their Lies*, 119.

224 Ibid., 143.

225 *Mein Kampf*, 324.

226 Martin Luther, and Teodore G. Tappert. "Letter on the Harsh Book," *Selected Writings of Martin Luther, Volume 1* (Fortress Press, 2007), 373.

227 Adolf Hitler, edited by Norman H. Baynes, *The Speeches of Adolf Hitler, April 1922-August 1939, Vol. 1* (Oxford University Press, 1942), 19–20.

228 William Shirer, *The Rise and Fall of the Third Reich* (New York: Simon & Schuster Paperbacks, 1990), 101.

229 The Bayreuth Festival is a seasonal music festival held annually since 1876 in Bayreuth, Bavaria featuring Wagner's operas.

230 Adolf Hitler, Sämtliche Aufzeichnung 1905–1924, 1034.

231 *Mein Kampf*, 16.

232 Ibid., 148.

233 August Kubizek, *The Young Hitler I Knew* (London: Greenhill Books, 2006), 185–188.

234 Ibid., 118.

235 Richard Wagner, *Correspondence of Wagner and Liszt* (New York: Haskell House Publishers, 1897), 145. Edited by William Ashton Ellis, Originally translated by Francis Hueffer.

236 *Judaism in Music* by Richard Wagner, Translated by William Ashton Ellis. All the passages of Judaism in Music are taken from *The Theatre, Richard Wagner's Prose Works, Volume 3* (London: Kegan Paul, Trench, Trubner & Co., 1894), 79–100.

237 *Judaism in Music*, 90–91.

238 Ibid.

239 *Richard Wagner's Prose Works Volume 6* (London: K. Paul, Trench, Trübner, 1897), 271.

240 Ibid., 268.

241 *Judaism in Music*, 82–83.

242 Ibid., 85.

243 Though Mozart was from Salzburg, Austria and lived in Venna until his death (1781–1791) in Austria, the Germanness of his music and his German identity expressed in his letters made him known as a German composer. Wagner seemed to consider Mozart as a great German composer.

244 *Judaism in Music*, 95–96.

245 Ibid., 99.

246 Ibid.

247 *Judaism in Music*, 100.

248 Criticism of Mendelssohn may come from Wagner's personal past resentments. Though Wagner respected Mendelssohn, Mendelssohn treated Wagner badly. In one incident Mendelssohn ignored an early symphony Wagner had sent to him. In another, Mendelssohn agreed to conduct the overture of *Tannihauser* at Wagner's opera in 1846, but it was disastrous and this upset Wagner very much.

249 *Old Testament*, Book of Esther 3:12–14.

250 On the other hand, at the ending of the book of Esther, Queen Esther's courage convinced King Ahasuerus to stop the genocide of the Jews. This story became the source of "Purim," the Jewish festival.

251 Adolf Hitler, *Sämtliche Aufzeichnungen: 1905–1924, 185*.

252 Ibid., 187.

253 Ibid., 197.

254 *Richard Wagner's Prose Works Volume 6* (London: K. Paul, Trench, Trübner,1897), 275–278.

255 Ibid., 284.

256 Ibid., 225.

257 Adolf Hitler, *Sämtliche Aufzeichnung 1905–1924, 186*. Original English translation used "Swastika" for the German word "Hakenkreuz."

258 *Oxford English Dictionary* second edition (1989), s.v. "Hakenkreuz."

259 *Webster's Seventh New Collegiate Dictionary* (1977), s.v. "Hakenkreuz."

260 http://www.etymonline.com, "Hakenkreuz" (accessed on January 12, 2012).

261 Christian Zentner and Friedemann Bedurftig, *The Encyclopedia of the Third Reich* (New York: Macmillan Publishing Company, 1991), 329.

262 Jacob Grimm and Wilhelm Grimm, *Deutsches Worterbuch* (Berlin: Verlag von S. Hirzel, 1877), s.v. "Hakenkreuz."

263 Hendrich Schliemann, *Ilios, Stadt und land der Trojaner* (Berlin: F.A. Brockhaus, 1881), 389, 390.

264 Guido von List, *Das Geheimnis der Runen* (Leipzig, Germany: E. F. Steinacker, 1908), 20.

265 Adolf Hitler, *Sämtliche Aufzeichnungen: 1905–1924* (Stuttgart, Deutsche: Verlags-Anstalt, 1980), 186. English translation is by Hasso Castrup. The author changed the word "Swastika" to "Hakenkreuz" in English translation to emphasize the original German.

266 Although there are several translations into English of *Mein Kampf*, the translation used here is by Ralph Manheim in 1943, which is the most widely read and used. Boldface emphasis provided by the author.

267 **Hakenkreuz** 1931, proper German name for the Nazi swastika (q.v.), lit. "hook-cross," from O.H.G. *hako* "hook," from P.Gmc. **hoka-*, from PIE **keg-* "hook, tooth" (http://www.etymonline.com).

268 Adolf Hitler, translated by Ralph Manheim. *Mein Kampf* (Boston: Houghton Mifflin, 1943), 496.

269 "Beer Hall Scene Gave Comic Opera Touch to Hitler Coup," *New York Times* (December 2, 1923).

270 "Prague Bans Wearing of Swastika," *New York Times* (March 25, 1932).

271 http://select.nytimes.com/gst/abstract.html?res=F30917FE3F5C16738DDD A00994DB405B838FF1D3 (accessed on January 15, 2012).

272 http://www.ldoceonline.com/dictionary/swastika (accessed on March 22, 2013).

273 All emphasis is the author's.

274 Thomas Wilson, *Swastika: The Earliest Known Symbol and Its Migrations* (United States National Museum. Report, 1894), 768. "The swastika has been called by different names in different countries, though nearly all countries have in later year accepted the ancient Sanskrit name of Swastika (svastika); and this name is recommended as the most definite and certain, being now the most general and, indeed, almost universal."

275 According to the *Oxford English Dictionary*, the first swastika appeared in English as the original positive meaning: 1871 ALABASRTER *Wheel of Law* 249 On the great toe is the Trisul. On each side of the others a Swastika.

276 According to the *Oxford English Dictionary*, the term "swastika" referring to the Nazi emblem first appeared: 1932 '*NORDICUS*' *Hitlerism* ii. 17 Thousands flocked to his standard—the 'Hakenkreuz'—(swastika), the ancient anti-Semitic cross in a color scheme of red-white-black in memory of the colors of the old army. The *New York Times* also used the word in a story published March 25, 1932, "Prague Bans Wearing of Swastika."

277 Abraham Joshua Heschel, *The Prophets* (Harper Collins, 2001), xxiv.

278 Booklet of *Report of the Hindu-Jewish* Leadership *Summit* (February 17–20, 2008), 9.

279 Adam Dickter, "ADL Downgrades Sswastika as Jewish Hate Symbol," *Jewish Week* (August 2, 2010).

280 Adam Dickter, "Growing-Up Hate in Jackson Heights: Swastikas at shul, public Libraries in Queens Neighborhood Seen as Malicious Attack Rather Than Kids' Prank," *Jewish Week* (November 11, 2011).

281 http://www.dnainfo.com/20120111/midtown/nypd-releases-video-of-midtown-swastika-suspects (accessed on January 22, 2012).

282 http://cityroom.blogs.nytimes.com/2011/11/11/cars-burned-and-swastikas-scrawled-in-brooklyn-jewish-area/ (accessed on January 22, 2012).

283 http://www.nbcnewyork.com/news/local/Swastikas-Burned-Cars-Insurance-Scam-Midwood-Brooklyn-137090188.html (accessed on January 22, 2012).

284 Rebbe Nachman of Breslow. *The Empty Chair: Finding Hope and Joy* (Woodstock: Jewish Light Publishing, 1994), 112.

285 *Jodoshinshu Seiten* (Kyoto: Hongwanji Shuppanbu 1988), 1436.

Figure Credits

Frontispiece photo by the author.

1 Photo by the author; Kyoto city map at Mapion.co.jp.

2–17 Photos by the author.

18 http://dearbooks.cafe.coocan.jp/wagara/kotoba09a.html (accessed on January 12, 2012) .

19 http://www.rakuten.ne.jp/gold/ ranma/ (accessed on January 12, 2012).

20 http://www2.harimaya.com/sengoku/bukemon.html (accessed on January 12, 2012).

21 http://www.asgy.co.jp/cgi-bin/kmnlist.pl?manji (accessed on January 12, 2012).

22 Drawing by the author.

23 Public domain photo. https://commons.wikimedia.org/wiki/File:Shaken.JPG.

24 Photo by the author.

25 Photo: courtesy of Anrakuju-in temple.

26 Photo by the author. 8th century, China (Harvard Art Museum).

27 Christian Luczantis, *The Buddhist Heritage of Pakistan: Art of Gandhara* (New York Asia Society, 2011).

28 Photo by the author.

29 Koryu-ji temple souvenir booklet.

30–33 Photos by the author.

34 The map is re-created by the author, based upon the Wilson's map.

35 Public Domain photo. https://en.wikipedia.org/wiki/File:HinduSwastika.svg.

36 Photo by World Image. Collection of seals of the Indus Civilization. JPG. https://commons.wikimedia.org/wiki/File:IndusValleySeals.JPG (accessed on January 21, 2018).

37 Photo courtesy of Jerry Pevahouse.

38 http://www.fullstopindia.com/10-important-symbols-of-hinduism (accessed on January 15, 2012).

39 Photo: courtesy of Dr. M. G. Prasad.

40–42 Photos by the author.

43 Photo courtesy of Ramzez Imaginative.

44 Photo by Bsalzberg. Mosaic at the synagogue at Ein Gedi. https://commons.wikimedia.org/wiki/File בלצ_סרק_ספיסבפב_המהשלב_הראשיו_שיל_בית_הכנסת.JPG.

45 Photo courtesy of Ramzez Imaginative.

46 Photo by Hagit Baldar. https://commons.wikimedia.org/wiki/File:OemElKanaatier_(9).JPG.

47 Drawing from Paul Carus, "Fylfot and Swastika," The Open Court (London: Open Court Publishing Co., 1902), 360.

48 Photo by Oosoom. https://commons.wikimedia.org/wiki/File:Bishop_Huyshe_Wolcott_Yeatman-Biggs_head.jpg.

49 Photo courtesy of Louise Barder.

50 Photo by the author.

51 Photo by Giovanni Dall'Orto https://commons.wikimedia.org/wiki/File:9821_-_Milano_-_Sant%27Ambrogio_-_Sarcofago_di_Stilicone_-_Foto_Giovanni_Dall%27Orto_25-Apr-2007.jpg,

52 Public domain photo. https://commons.wikimedia.org/wiki/File:Sunny_Beach_Nesebar_centre_2.jpg.

53 Photo by the author (Metropolitan Museum of Art, New York).

54 Drawing by the author (*left*) and public domain photo (*right*): https://commons.wikimedia.org/wiki/File:Skastika_symbol_in_the_window_of_Lalibela_Rock_hewn_churches.jpg.

55, 56 Photos by the author (Metropolitan Museum of Art, New York).

57 Photo by the author (Harvard Art Museum).

58 http://www.stormfront.org/forum/t730136/ (accessed on January 15, 2012).

59 http://www.paulstravelblog.com/2008/05/shia-islam.html (accessed on January 16, 2012).

60 http://www.crystallography.fr/mathcryst/pdf/istanbul/Necefoglu_slides.pdf (accessed on August 31, 2013).

61 http://mise-en-trope.blogspot.com (accessed on January 16, 2012).

62 Photo courtesy of Rev. Shofu Banchi.

63 https://www.advantour.com/uzbekistan/khiva/tash-hovli.htm (accessed on January 22, 2018).

64 Bruce Willis, The Adinkra Dictionary (Washington DC The Pyramid Complex, 1998), 142.

65 Public domain photo. https://commons.wikimedia.org/wiki/File:GhanaSwastika.jpg.

66 Photo by the author (Metropolitan Museum of Art, New York).

67 Public Domain Photo. https://commons.wikimedia.org/wiki/File:NASA-SpiralGalaxyM101-20140505.jpg.

68 Photo by the author. Courtesy of the owner, Jerry Pevahouse.

69 Photo by the author (National Museum of the American Indian, New York, NY).

70 Photo by the author. The author's personal collection (gift of Mr. and Mrs. Gene Erickson).

71 Public domain photo. https://commons.wikimedia.org/wiki/File:Collection_of_thirteen_pieces_of_Navajo_Indian_silver_jewelry_on_display,_ca.1900_(CHS-4059).jpg.

72 Public domain photo. https://commons.wikimedia.org/wiki/File:Native_American_basketball_team.jpg.

73 http://lumq.com/02/swasika/ (accessed on January 18, 2012).

74 http://www.gothicnews.com/boy-scout-swastika/ (accessed on January 18, 2012).

75 http://lumq.com/02/swasika/ (accessed on January 18, 2012).

76 Public domain photo. https://en.wikipedia.org/wiki/Fernie_Swastikas#/media/File:Fernie_Swastikas_hockey_team_1922.jpg

77 http://www.vnnforum.com/showthread.php?p=1352840 (accessed on January 18, 2012).

78 http://digitalgallery.nypl.org/nypldigital/dgkeysearchdetail.cfm?trg=1&strucID=715099&imageID=831845 (accessed on January 12, 2012).

79 Public domain photo. https://commons.wikimedia.org/wiki/File:Swastika_ON.JPG.

80–82 Photos by the author.

83 Courtesy of the owner of the book, Masumi Kikuchi.

84 http://www.janm.org/collections/item/99.201.25/, http://www.janm.org/collections/item/99.201.12/ (accessed on January 18, 2012).

85 http://www.janm.org/collections/item/99.201.10/ (accessed on January 18, 2012).

86 http://www.janm.org/collections/item/99.201.27/ (accessed on January 18, 2012).

87–89 Photos by the author.

90 http://michelduchaine.com/tag/adolf-lanz/ (accessed on March 1, 2015).

91 http://peter-diem.at/Buchtexte/hakenkreuz.htm (accessed on March 1, 2015).

92 http://www.crystalinks.com/thule.html (accessed on January 21, 2012).

93 The image was created by the author with his computer.

94 Public domain photo. https://commons.wikimedia.org/wiki/File:Flag_of_the_NSDAP_(1920%E2%80%931945).svg.

95 Photo courtesy of Kazue Ishiyama.

96 http://www.freewebs.com/manwomans/apps/photos/ photo?photoid=25308572 (accessed on January 21, 2012).

97 Public domain photos. https://commons.wikimedia.org/wiki/File:Bristol_Blenheim_Mk._IV_of_the_Finnish_Air_Force.jpg and https://commons.wikimedia.org/wiki/File:Flag_of_Finland_Air_force_squadrons_without_squadron_emblem.svg.

98 http://rmarkmusser.com/eco-fascism (accessed on December 21, 2017).

99 http://www.moonwheel-historical.com/product_info.php?products_id=1289 (accessed on January 21, 2012).

100 Public domain photo. https://commons.wikimedia.org/wiki/File:DR_1934_530_Luftpost.jpg.

101 Public domain photo. https://commons.wikimedia.org/wiki/File:GermanCrossInGold WithDiamonds.jpg.

102 Public domain photo. https://commons.wikimedia.org/wiki/File:DE_Band_mit_RK_(1).jpg.

103 Public domain photo. https://commons.wikimedia.org/wiki/File:War_Ensign_of_Germany_(1935–1938).svg.

104 Public domain photo. https://commons.wikimedia.org/wiki/File:Deutsches_Reich_Mother%27s_Cross_of_Honour.jpg.

105 Public domain photo. https://commons.wikimedia.org/wiki/File:Deutsche-Christen-flag.jpg.

About the Author

Rev. Dr. T. K. Nakagaki is a Buddhist priest, ordained in the 750-year-old Jodoshinshu tradition of Japanese Buddhism. He was ordained at the Nishi Hongwanji Temple in Kyoto, Japan, in 1980. He graduated from Ryukoku University in Kyoto, majoring in Buddhist History in 1983, and later conducted advanced study in Jodoshinshu Buddhist doctrine at Gyoshin Buddhist Seminary in Osaka, Japan, from 1983 to 1985. He received an M.A. in Linguistics from California State University at Fresno in 1994 and earned a Doctorate of Ministry in Multifaith Studies from the New York Theological Seminary in 2012.

Rev. Dr. Nakagaki is a Founder and President of Heiwa Peace and Reconciliation Foundation of New York, and current executive officer and former President of the Buddhist Council of New York, Hiroshima Peace Ambassador, Peace Correspondent of Nagasaki City, Community Clergy Liaison for the NYC Police Department, and former Vice President of the Interfaith Center of New York. He served as a resident priest for Jodoshinshu Buddhist communities in Seattle from 1985 to 1989, in Parlier, California, from 1989 to 1994, and at the New York Buddhist Church from 1994 to 2010.

Since 1994, Rev. Nakagaki has organized an annual interfaith peace event to commemorate the Hiroshima and Nagasaki atomic bombings, and from 2002 to 2011 he organized the annual 9/11 WTC Memorial Floating Lanterns Ceremony. He is the author of three books in Japanese, *A New York Buddhist Priest Walks in India* (Gendai Shokan, 2003); *Diary of a Manhattan Monk* (Gendai Shokan, 2010); and *Manji and Hakenkreuz* (Gendaishokan, 2013) He is also a noted Japanese calligrapher.

E-mail: tknakagaki@gmail.com
Address: P.O. Box 20405, Floral Park, NY 11002-0405